Interpreting Immigration at Museums and Historic Sites

Interpreting History

SERIES EDITOR

Rebecca K. Shrum, Indiana University–Purdue University Indianapolis

MANAGING EDITOR

Bob Beatty, AASLH

EDITORIAL BOARD

About the Series

The American Association for State and Local History publishes the *Interpreting History* series in order to provide expert, in-depth guidance in interpretation for history professionals at museums and historic sites. The books are intended to help practitioners expand their interpretation to be more inclusive of the range of American history.

Books in this Series:

- help readers quickly learn about the questions surrounding a specific topic,
- introduce readers to the challenges of interpreting this part of history, and
- highlight best practice examples of how interpretation has been done by different organizations.

They enable institutions to place their interpretative efforts into a larger context, despite each having a specific and often localized mission. These books serve as quick references to practical considerations, further research, and historical information.

Titles in the Series

Interpreting Immigration at Museums and Historic Sites

Edited by Dina A. Bailey

AASLH

AMERICAN ASSOCIATION for STATE and LOCAL HISTORY

ROWMAN & LITTLEFIELD
Lanham • Boulder • New York • London

Published by Rowman & Littlefield
An imprint of The Rowman & Littlefield Publishing Group, Inc.
4501 Forbes Boulevard, Suite 200, Lanham, Maryland 20706
www.rowman.com

Unit A, Whitacre Mews, 26-34 Stannary Street, London SE11 4AB, United Kingdom

British Library Cataloguing in Publication Information Available

Library of Congress Cataloging-in-Publication Data

Includes bibliographic references and index.
ISBN 978-1-4422-6323-9 (cloth : alk. paper)
ISBN 978-1-4422-6324-6 (pbk. : alk. paper)
ISBN 978-1-4422-6325-3 (electronic)

∞™ The paper used in this publication meets the minimum requirements of American National Standard for Information Sciences—Permanence of Paper for Printed Library Materials, ANSI/NISO Z39.48-1992.

Printed in the United States of America

To realize the American dream, the most important thing to understand is that it belongs to everybody. It's a human dream. If you understand this and work very hard, it is possible.

—Cristina Saralegui

This book is dedicated to those who dream.

CONTENTS

CONTENTS

ACKNOWLEDGMENTS

I would like to extend my deepest gratitude to all of the contributors who believed in this book and kept the faith throughout the journey. Now, perhaps more than ever before, it is important for us to find spaces to have authentic dialogues that bring us closer together rather than farther apart. The authors who contributed to this book made these spaces available in their own communities; their museums opened their doors and actively participated in authentic efforts to collaborate. In particular, I would like to acknowledge the hard work of contributing author Sarah Pharaon, who originally brought all of the contributors together. This book would not have been published without her vision and leadership. As the senior director of methodology and practice at the International Coalition of Sites of Conscience, Sarah Pharaon knew the relevance and timeliness of finding productive ways for communities to dialogue about immigration in the United States. Finally, I would like to acknowledge the intentions of each of you reading this book; as Confucius said so long ago, "A journey of a thousand miles begins with a single step." Thank you for walking alongside the authors of this book as we continue this journey.

INTRODUCTION

Using Dialogue to Interpret Immigration: The National Dialogues on Immigration Project

Sarah Pharaon

In January 2014, as the culmination of a process that began in 2008, twenty members of the International Coalition of Sites of Conscience launched the National Dialogues on Immigration Project, a cross-regional series of purposefully structured, facilitated dialogue programs designed to engage more than twenty thousand visitors of all ages in a new national conversation on critical immigration topics. Using their collections and capitalizing on their unique historical spaces and exhibitions, each of the twenty museums utilized stories from their own history as starting points to open dialogue on immigration, past and present.[1] To link the twenty local programs into a larger national discussion, as well as to share resources and learning across regions, the project developed branded marketing materials as well as an online website featuring a timeline of immigration and civil rights history, contemporary policy information, and opportunities for civic action as well as twenty dialogue program models in order to enable replication by interested stakeholders across the country. In undertaking this work, the twenty museums and historic sites involved, reenvisioned their institutions as active public forums. They attempted to change the public perception of museums as "temples of knowledge" in which guides and exhibitions passively educate their visitors on the experiences of immigrants past and endeavored to serve as spaces in which visitors could share their own experiences, opinions, and assumptions about immigration today in an effort to promote personal and collective learning.

This was not a programmatic shift that these museums and historic sites undertook lightly. Museums involved in the project were hesitant to address issues of contemporary immigration in their communities for a number of reasons: a desire to avoid community conflict, a hesitancy to upset longstanding board members, and, most notably, concerns that funders would have reservations about programming that would be seen as too political in nature.[2] The launch of the National Dialogues on Immigration Project represents a substantial investment of time, resources, and finances by all twenty project participants as well as the larger membership and leadership of the International Coalition of Sites of Conscience. This introduction attempts to document the history of the National Dialogues on Immigration Project and the lessons learned throughout its six-year development in preparation for the reading of the upcoming chapters of this book.

Launched in 1999, the International Coalition of Sites of Conscience is a network of historic sites and community-centered museums dedicated to using the power of place as leverage to foster dialogue on contemporary social issues. In fifteen years, the coalition has grown from its founding nine members to include over 250 member sites in fifty-five countries. Management of this rapid growth has been facilitated through the development of seven regional networks, allowing the coalition to move forward globally while working within the unique social and historical contexts of each region. Six of the seven regional networks have historically organized their work around a contemporary social issue shared across the nations represented within their network.

Sites in the African Regional Network, for example, have concentrated their collaborative work on their shared dedication toward remembering and building on histories of colonialism and slavery. The Latin American Network works collaboratively to preserve the memory of those detained, tortured, and executed under dictatorial regimes and demand accountability from governments loathe to recognize these dark years of national and regional history. Sites in the Middle East and North Africa attempt to document history as it happens, working together to share practices in the wake of renewed violence and human rights struggles. European sites have organized around their desire to understand how difference, exclusion, and xenophobia manifest, whether in Nazi Germany, the 1990s Balkans conflict, or discrimination against the Roma people today. The Russian Sites of Conscience Network raises awareness of the history and consequences of totalitarianism to actively engage citizens in addressing threats to Russian democracy today. The mission of the Asian Sites of Conscience Network is "to confront growing religious extremism by engaging young people of all faiths in exploring their countries' histories of repression, ethnic conflict, and violence to find new paths toward tolerance and peace."[3] Having a common focus for their collaborative work has served each of these networks well, allowing them to produce shared educational resources, advise each other on best practices, and grow their regional membership to include new sites seeking guidance and mentorship on how they might better address the issue at hand.

By contrast, the coalition's North American Network, comprising sites in Canada and the United States, was not established with one thematic focus for its work. By 2007, the network had grown to include over fifty sites that were extremely diverse in the contemporary issues they hoped to address. Sites across the United States were working to foster dialogue on a variety of topics ranging from the legacies of forced incarceration (Bosque Redondo, Fort Sumner, New Mexico) to sex trafficking (Matilda Joslyn Gage Foundation, Fayetteville, New York) to racial equity (National Civil Rights Museum, Memphis, Tennessee). Though these sites were invested in the coalition and its methodology, most labored on their own without the assistance of a strong internal network and without a common peer-established purpose. In 2007, through conference calls and email discussions, members of the North American Network launched efforts to choose a theme that some, if not all, could work collaboratively to address.

At the same time, growing numbers of new immigrants, propelled by a fruitful economy, were settling in communities across the United States, in some cases resulting in the demographic transformation of small cities and rural areas.[4] This number was also propelled by unprecedented growth in undocumented immigration. By 2007, there were an estimated twelve million undocumented immigrants in the United States, the peak number recorded for a population that had been rising for decades.[5] As part of its plan to address this growth, the federal government passed the Secure Fence Act, authorizing the building of a seven-hundred-mile border fence between the United States and Mexico. The Comprehensive Immigration Reform Act of 2007, providing legal status and a path to citizenship for the approximately twelve to twenty million undocumented immigrants residing in the United States while increasing border enforcement, failed to win congressional support. The contentious debates that arose around such legislation all too often reinforced stereotypes and divided communities. The Southern Poverty Law Center cited the vitriolic immigration debate as one of the primary causes of the more than 50 percent increase in hate groups in the United States since 2000.[6] In this climate there was an urgent need for new spaces where Americans, including new immigrants, could engage in informed and open dialogue across difference on the enduring and sensitive issue of immigration. Against this backdrop, the coalition secretariat, eight staff members who oversaw the larger work of the coalition, and a select group of its members began to explore whether immigration might be the unifying thematic topic they were looking for.

In 2008, the coalition brought together thirteen members representing diverse immigration histories and experiences, including the Angel Island Immigration Station Foundation (San Francisco, California), Arab American National Museum (Dearborn, Michigan), Chicago Cultural Alliance (Chicago, Illinois), Ellis Island Immigration Museum (New York, New York), Jane Addams Hull-House Museum (Chicago, Illinois), Japanese American National Museum (Los Angeles, California), Levine Museum of the New South (Charlotte, North Carolina), Lowell National Historic Park (Lowell, Massachusetts), Lower East Side Tenement Museum (New York, New York), New Americans Museum (San Diego, California), Save Ellis Island (Budd Lake, New Jersey), Tsongas Industrial History Center (Lowell, Massachusetts), and Wing Luke Museum of the Asian Pacific American Experience (Seattle, Washington). From August 8 to 13, 2008, sites met at the Lower East Side Tenement Museum, the Pocantico Conference Center of the Rockefeller Brothers Fund, and the Ellis Island Immigration Museum in an ongoing series of events designed to:

- build the capacity of museum staff to implement dialogue programs focused on immigration issues within their respective communities;

- enable participants to share and disseminate program models, evaluation strategies, and resources;

- foster collaboration and exchange among museums tackling similar issues;

- develop joint media outreach strategies that encourage citizens to get involved in contemporary immigration issues; and

- enable a better understanding of immigration policy issues and how to create resources that encourage learning about these issues.[7]

During their time together, the sites identified three characteristics of the larger immigration debate that they hoped to mitigate through their work together. These challenges, though initially raised by sites as issues of local concern to their specific communities, were found to be shared in common by many if not all of the attending sites. First, site representatives agreed that national and local immigration discourse had "devolved into a state which promoted misinformation and demagoguery."[8] As part of this conversation, attendees discussed the heightened attention given to the commentary of political pundits like Lou Dobbs and reviewed news articles and opinion pieces published in the regions in which their sites were located. In further support of this observation, sites like the Arab American National Museum, whose community was still grappling with a rise in violence against its members after the attacks of September 11, 2001, shared stories of racial profiling gathered from the national listening sessions they organized for the museum's opening in 2005. Site representatives from the New Americans Museum discussed safety procedures they put in place for staff members after San Diego residents protested the museum's existence and threatened violence against its staff before the museum had even opened its doors.

Attendees also agreed that access to American democracy was limited for many; democracy was in effect exclusionary, allowing for those with the highest levels of economic standing to have a stronger voice in the democratic process through campaign donations, lobbying efforts, and marketing campaigns. Even the act of voting, said some participants, was unequally practiced among the ethnic and racial populations comprising the visitors to their sites. Raising this point was particularly important for the Wing Luke Museum of the Asian Pacific American Experience that had just closed a community-curated temporary exhibit on civic engagement in the Asian American community during which voter participation drives were held in the museum's gallery spaces (photo 0.1). Finally, site representatives agreed that the debate was being dominated by staunchly anti-immigrant voices or voices from unabashed immigrant advocacy organizations. When examining the media's coverage of current immigration trends, there was a dearth of moderate voices within the conversation. As participant Lisa Lee, director of the Jane Addams Hull-House Museum, summarized, those whose opinions and beliefs didn't align completely with either of the extreme perspectives, "the middle 50%, is just not participating."[9]

To address these concerns, site representatives sought to develop a programmatic strategy that would allow for diverse contemporary perspectives to be shared against the backdrop of historic facts about immigration and related issues. Attendees agreed that, in order to inspire people to become active participants in shaping immigration issues and dispelling misinformation and stereotype, they needed to engage their visitors in a form

Photo 0.1.   Visitors at the Wing Luke Museum of the Asian Pacific American Experience.
The Wing Luke Museum of the Asian Pacific American Experience.

of learning and exchange that models and supports active participation: "They recognized that traditional museum exhibit and education formats based on passive learning often encourage passive behavior, not active participation."[10] Site representatives explored a variety of ways to model active civic engagement in museums so that visitors could continue that engagement when they left the site. One of the interpretative methodologies they discussed was a specific communication process called facilitated dialogue. While together at the Pocantico Conference Center, site representatives received substantial methodological training from dialogue facilitator Tammy Bormann. Following the training, the sites agreed to develop and pilot facilitated programs that would be intentionally designed to educate people through dialogue, a process defined by Bormann at the training as a constructed experience in which participants "share their ideas, information, experiences, and assumptions for the purposes of personal and collective learning."[11]

One of numerous interpretative approaches, facilitated dialogue is a specific strategy that enables visitors to make sense of larger historical themes through an examination of their own experiences and assumptions as well as those of other visitors to the site. It asks program participants to abandon the premise that only museum staff will act as educators and instead embraces the philosophy that all program participants have vital information and experiences to share with each other. In this model, museum staff serve as facilitators, working to build a nonhierarchical experience that can enable deeper communal learning than the traditional "educator relays information to visitor" model. International Coalition of Sites of Conscience members apply this framework to enduring social issues addressed by museums to foster an exchange of ideas, seeking to achieve what Americans for the Arts's Animating Democracy Initiative defines as "deliberate, sustained, informed communication on complex and multi-dimensional issues that are of concern to multiple segments of a community and that elicit multiple and often conflicting perspectives."[12]

Facilitated dialogue as an interpretive approach also builds on the fact that, as trusted educational and community spaces making human connections to the past, museums and historic sites are ideal venues for fostering dialogue and civic engagement. There has been growing recognition of the need for museums to serve in this capacity, as is evidenced in publications such as the American Association of Museums's groundbreaking *Mastering Civic Engagement* in 2002 and the 2007 launch of the journal *Museums and Social Issues*, dedicated to exploring the contemporary role museums might play in fostering dialogue around the social issues of their communities.

Through member programs at historic sites around the world, the coalition has identified a variety of different dialogue models that move visitors beyond passive learning, engaging them in sharing perspectives and experiences on issues of shared concern. Many of the coalition's dialogue programs are carefully designed and facilitated to follow an "arc of dialogue": a sequence of questions designed to address sensitive issues by building the conversation gradually. In a museum-based arc of dialogue, visitors first participate in a common experience, most often a tour, gallery walk, school activity, or lecture. The fact that all participants share the experience together serves to break down hierarchies of prior knowledge of the topic; everyone at least knows the body of information to which they have just been exposed. Facilitators then work from a carefully designed process of questions, asking participants to first share personal experiences, then identify common experiences, then move to larger and more complex issues before moving toward synthesis and closure. The arc is designed to build trust and establish constructive communication that allows participants to interact with history in more relevant and personal ways. As an example, in one immigration-based facilitated dialogue program, the interpretive staff of Lowell National Historical Park designed a walking tour that used an arc of dialogue to help their local community (in which one in five residents is a first-generation immigrant)[13] wrestle "with questions of who has access to 'Americanness' in a constantly evolving political landscape."[14] Against the geographic backdrop of a statue honoring immigrants who toiled in the Lowell Mills, Lowell City Hall, and the local high school, facilitators asked visitors questions from an arc of dialogue that included the following:

- What do you say when you are asked, "Where are you from?"
- Did anyone have multiple answers to this question or struggle to answer?
- Based on your own community or experiences, what makes an "immigrant" neighborhood?

- How has immigration shaped economic activity or institutions in your community?

- What knowledge or skills, if any, do you think make people American?

- What does being an American mean to you?

Facilitators interspersed the questions with historical content about the immigrant history of Lowell and the role that the locations on the walking tour route have played in defining and facilitating Lowell's growth.[15]

The arc of dialogue model was not entirely new to all of the sites in attendance at the 2008 meeting. Some of the sites that had been members of the coalition for a longer period of time had prior experience in developing facilitated dialogue programs. For example, at the Jane Addams Hull-House Museum, facilitated dialogue helped visitors use history to explore the development of social welfare programs. Visitors touring the site were asked to select one object that particularly resonated with them (items range from a soup can that would have been used in the communal kitchen to a copy of the FBI's file on Jane Addams herself) and explain why it had particular meaning to them. After sharing these personal connections with the site and its history, visitors explored how their experiences at Hull-House added to their understanding of the local story of Chicago, how the ability of individuals to access social services today was similar or different from Jane Addams's day, and how they defined "underserved communities" today. Deciding to use dialogue as the core approach behind new programs on immigration was an easy choice for Hull-House and for others at the table with similar programmatic experience. By contrast, sites like the Ellis Island Immigration Museum were meeting fellow coalition members for the first time at this gathering and had little experience with facilitated dialogic methodology. Piloting a dialogue program at their sites felt intimidating and would be a more challenging endeavor. Thus the coalition secretariat committed to provide additional interpretive training throughout the next year at three regional meetings in the Northeast, Midwest, and West Coast.

In embracing facilitated dialogue as an interpretive technique and committing to pilot new dialogue programs around contemporary immigration, the group unanimously decided to launch the Immigration Sites of Conscience Network with the following statement:

> We are diverse institutions coming from very different contexts and working in different ways. We pledge to help each other to use historical perspective and heritage to create new opportunities for education and dialogue on today's immigration issues among people with diverse perspective and backgrounds. Our programs will be designed to: stimulate and elevate the ongoing local and national conversation on immigration and its related issues; address misinformation and stereotypes; promote humanitarian values; and, treat all audiences as stakeholders in the immigration dialogue. In this way, we aim to promote a more inclusive, participatory democracy.[16]

Ever conscious of whose voices were being excluded even within their own internal discussions, the network's original thirteen member sites were concerned about the lack of historically African American sites at the meeting. In response to this concern, the coalition secretariat committed "to organize a second leadership seminar by the fall of 2009 for civil rights history museums to address the specific conflicts and opportunities inspired by the explosion in recent immigration in historically black/white communities in the Southeast." The group went on to point out that "civil rights museums are in a unique position to use their historic legacy of protest and action to inspire discussion on current issues in communities across the United States."[17]

Almost a year later, from June 25 to 28, 2009, the coalition brought together a group of civil rights museum representatives, leaders from the Immigration Sites of Conscience Network, and national immigration advocates to the National Civil Rights Museum (Memphis, Tennessee) to explore the museums' interests in using their reach and resources to position contemporary immigration as a civil rights issue. As sites eager to engage burgeoning immigrant and receiving communities throughout the Southeast, the group gathered to explore if these museums could be places to connect divided communities of immigrants and longer-rooted Americans of all races. Participants sought to identify specific concerns and conflicts around immigration in their communities, identify issues and audiences that immigration advocates are interested in addressing and reaching via partnerships with civil rights museums, and generate ideas for how attendees might combine the existing strengths and resources of civil rights museums and immigration advocates to reach new audiences.[18] Participants identified five key issues shared in common and commonly voiced by members of both new immigrant populations and civil rights museum audiences:

- Immigration issues are related to class, color, and language.

- The legacy of Jim Crow laws and institutional racism in the United States affects all communities of color, particularly in residential housing patterns, school segregation, incarceration rates, and the digital divide (unequal access to technology).

- There is unequal access to services in the areas of health care and education.

- Racial profiling and hate crimes are on the rise in communities of color.

- There is limited education around immigration in the Southeast to combat ignorance.[19]

Attendees agreed that all five issues offered the opportunity to work in coalition with each other and brainstormed ideas for how they might bring people together, including "Know Your Rights" programs (workshops that provide communities with training on what their rights are in the United States and how to combat abuse in their communities), "Strangers No Longer" programs (opportunities for people from different backgrounds to interact in new contexts, like museum spaces), and programs for parents of school-aged children (which would use the historical struggles of education access at sites like Central High School in Little Rock, Arkansas, as a platform to explore how parents might advocate for better schools today).[20]

Evaluation results from the seminar were overwhelmingly positive. Immigration advocates, like Isabel Rubio, executive director of the Hispanic Interest Coalition of Alabama (HICA), appreciated that these meetings weren't held under the all too often used "how do we increase and diversify our museum attendance" notion of community engagement, but rather to propel organizations' mutual interests in addressing local issues. Ms. Rubio stated that:

> this opportunity has given so much credibility to the issue of immigration that was hard to get across to the museum folks in our community. . . . We came to the workshop as equal partners and the museum saw us in a different light. They recognize the value that we offer and opened communication in a way that we didn't have before. It has opened their eyes, increased our credibility with them and gives me hope for a better future.[21]

Ms. Rubio and the staff at the Birmingham Civil Rights Institute (Birmingham, Alabama) returned to their community committed to working together. In the weeks immediately following the Memphis gathering, the Birmingham Civil Rights Institute agreed to keep their site open after hours so that adult students from HICA's English as a Second Language program could attend the museum with their families.

As the final item on their agenda, the museums committed to joining the original members of the Immigration Sites of Conscience Network. The network was rebranded to reflect this change as the Immigration and Civil Rights Sites of Conscience Network. These new members recognized that they had a unique opportunity to provide safe spaces where new immigrants and receiving communities could come together. However, they also recognized that this role was qualitatively different from how many of them were currently operating. In order to be successful in this role, sites requested additional training on contemporary immigration issues facing the nation and affecting their local communities, dialogic methodology training, and communication strategies to optimize stakeholder involvement.

The thirteen sites that launched the network in 2008 were simultaneously coming to the same conclusion. Between their initial gathering and the 2009 Memphis workshop, most network members launched pilot facilitated dialogue programs on immigration. The Levine Museum of the New South offered *Speaking of Change*, a program that used their temporary exhibition, *Changing Places*—which explored the history and traditions of both new and longtime Charlotte residents—as the starting point for group dialogues among civic leaders, city administrators, journalists, and religious leaders on addressing the city's growing cultural diversity. Ellis Island's program *Speaking of Immigration* used dialogic tours of the site's registration building and its yet-to-be-restored outbuildings to explore how federal officials implemented immigration policy a century ago and then asked participants to explore what values should drive the nation's current immigration policy in 2009 (photo 0.2).

As sites developed and tested their facilitated dialogue programs with museum audiences, the coalition was also able to gather significant data about what historical themes were most effective in promoting multiple perspectives and engaging audiences in dialogue across racial and ethnic lines. Sites also demonstrated that immigration concerns within their communities were dynamic and evolving as new conflicts flared or new

Photo 0.2. Ellis Island.
International Coalition of Sites of Conscience.

immigrant populations emerged. As a result, they concluded that effective facilitated dialogue programs must not only draw on the historical scholarship of the site, but must also respond to emerging issues within the immigration debate. Finally, while all but one site was able to successfully complete pilot programs, they (like their new civil rights museum colleagues) requested additional tools and resources to institutionalize facilitated dialogue programs at the site, including a toolkit of historical moments and themes, which would help contextualize contemporary immigration issues for their visitors; dialogic training for additional members of their staff; and training in evaluation methodology: How could they tell that these new facilitated dialogue programs were helping them meet their institutional goals?

In September 2010, the National Endowment for the Humanities awarded the coalition a planning grant to develop new approaches designed to open discussion and address visitors' underlying concerns and questions around immigration past and present. To do so, the coalition worked closely with humanities scholars, dialogue facilitation experts, and leading members of the Immigration and Civil Rights Sites of Conscience. In early 2011, the planning team met to identify humanities themes and historical moments they felt had the strongest potential for fostering dialogue between new immigrants and receiving communities. Team members began by reviewing the results of visitor surveys conducted at the Japanese American National Museum,

Levine Museum of the New South, Lower East Side Tenement Museum, National Civil Rights Museum, and the Wing Luke Museum of the Asian Pacific American Experience. These surveys asked questions such as:

- Do you feel well-informed about contemporary immigration issues in your community?

- From what sources do you obtain information regarding contemporary immigration issues?

- How closely do you feel immigration policy affects you?

- Do you think that immigration today is similar to immigration of the past?

- What issues around immigration are of the most importance to you?

- Do you think this museum is a good place to discuss immigration?

- What historical perspective on immigration would you most like to explore when you visit this museum?[22]

Overwhelmingly, visitors surveyed obtained information on contemporary immigration from the media, most commonly through television news, newspapers, and the web. At the same time, nearly 82 percent of the audience members surveyed indicated that museums were good places to discuss immigration. The staff of the National Civil Rights Museum was particularly surprised to see that over 60 percent of their visitors thought immigration-based programming would be a natural fit for the museum, that 25 percent "hadn't thought of it before," and that only 15 percent of their visitors responded that the museum should not discuss immigration. As one visitor responded, "immigration and its resulting discrimination is a continuation of civil rights and ultimately human rights issues."[23]

Citing results like these as evidence of the need for museums to serve as community centers for exploring immigration within a broader historical context, the planning team discussed the following:

- What do these survey results tell us about the historical truths that shape a visitor's understanding of immigration *and* about the historical truths that must be included in new program designs to support the visitor's learning about contemporary immigration?

- How can new historic scholarship promote open and effective dialogue and build on museums' historical assets to bridge divides across communities rather than reinforcing them?

- What interpretive and pedagogical strategies can best foster dialogue across difference and include communities that have been marginalized from conversations on immigration?

11

- What exhibition and programmatic tools can we develop to connect local visitors to historical resources and contemporary conversations in order to build a more effective national understanding of and exchange on immigration?[24]

While members of the planning team were focused on identifying historic scholarship and pedagogical strategies that would open dialogue on immigration in new and effective ways, the coalition also received funding from the Institute of Museum and Library Services to support the work of the Immigration and Civil Rights Sites of Conscience Regional Training Project. The project was designed to "build the skills of participating museum staff and the capacity of museums interpreting immigration histories to serve as new centers for public dialogue on pressing immigration issues of greatest concern to their communities."[25]

Responding to regionally specific differences in the immigration contexts and community populations of coalition member sites, the project established two peer-supported networks—one in the American Southeast and one in the American Southwest. Throughout the project, twenty participating museums, including civil rights museums that joined the network at the 2009 meeting and new members throughout the American Southwest, received training in designing and facilitating dialogue programs in adherence with the arc of dialogue model. They also met with marketing and communications experts to discuss how best to describe facilitated dialogue programs for their audiences. Participants also worked with evaluation consultant Conny Graft, who helped the sites define what successful community dialogue would look like at their sites and developed tools by which to help them assess this. Finally, participants met with national scholars and community leaders to hear current immigration research and discuss the ongoing debates in their regions. Throughout the three-year training initiative, eighteen of the twenty museums involved in the project piloted and evaluated dialogues on immigration at their sites.

When examining the substantial training and programmatic work completed from 2008 to 2013 in preparation for the 2014 launch of the National Dialogues on Immigration Project, Immigration and Civil Rights Sites of Conscience Network members and advisors identified four key points of learning: there is a lack of safe spaces for immigrants and receiving community members to speak about immigration issues together; the "America is a nation of immigrants" narrative does not work toward fostering enhanced understanding; branding immigration dialogue programs correctly is vital to a program's success; and facilitated dialogue on contentious social issues isn't easy, but finding "your people" helps. Each of these four points of learning is discussed below.

A Lack of Safe Spaces

Throughout all phases of the project, museum staff members and project advisors had rich conversations as to what the role of museums should be in helping elevate the public discourse on contemporary immigration. Substantial meeting time was given toward defining the purpose of museums in engaging their communities in facilitated dialogue around social issues. Ultimately, sites decided that it was not their goal to "change opinions," but, rather, to help visitors think differently about what they already knew by providing information on the history of immigration and creating a safe physical space in which to discuss their opinions on contemporary immigration issues with others.

As indicated through the project's formative evaluation surveys, museum visitors typically learned about immigration issues through various mediums, including learning gained through schooling and personal experience, but more commonly through newspapers, magazines, online media, and television. Visitor responses also showed a propensity given to educational "niche-ing"—receiving the vast majority of information from one media source, which in turn limits the variety of perspectives any individual might be exposed to.[26] At the same time, visitors indicated that they simply weren't talking to others about immigration. As one museum staff member said, "As a result of doing the dialogues I learned something about our community—that no one else is doing dialogues."[27] When asked how often they discussed immigration with family and/or friends, 22 percent of respondents indicated that they "never" or "almost never" did so. In results perhaps more telling, 70 percent of respondents said that they discussed immigration with others (those outside of their immediate circle of friends and family) only "every once in a while."[28] This lack of person-to-person connection poses real challenges to addressing immigration issues in the United States. Although studies consistently point to group contact between ethnic and racial groups as a proven method of reducing prejudice,[29] in geographic areas with large numbers of immigrants, economically segregated residential communities, work places, and schools often actually prevent contact between groups.

Faced with these behavioral patterns, museum staff involved in the project were concerned about the possibilities for facilitated dialogue on immigration at their sites. If visitors wouldn't talk about it with friends and family, why would they talk about it with strangers? One staff member said, "I really did not know if anyone would show up when we did our first dialogue and I was shocked when I saw that lots of people came and were eager to talk about this issue."[30] Was it possible that the problem wasn't that people didn't want to talk about immigration, but rather that the political climate had become so vitriolic that visitors felt uncomfortable doing so? If the answer was yes, then what museum staff needed to create was a space for visitors to explore the issues free from rhetoric.

In their 1998 study, Roy Rosenzweig and David Thelen found that "Americans put more trust in history museums and historic sites than in any other source for exploring the past."[31] This sense of protected public trust and this unique ability of sites to foster a safe space for discussion was commented on consistently in the evaluation of immigration dialogues. Many visitors "commented on how much they appreciated having a safe space to talk about immigration issues. In addition, visitors stated that for many of them this was the first time they heard someone 'different from them' talk about their immigration experiences and opinions."[32] However, it was not only hearing differing perspectives that was valuable to visitors. Respondents echoed the sentiments expressed by one participant who said, "this experience was valuable to me because not only did I learn others' ideas, I learned about my own ideas and where I stood with the topic."[33] This was reflected in the overall visitor survey results as well—over 80 percent of participants indicated that the dialogues helped them see immigration from a different perspective. Because the network had established its goal for these public dialogue programs as "helping visitors think differently about what they already knew," comments like this were clear markers of success. Though an unintentional outcome, many sites saw repeat visitation within their dialogue programs. As one museum staff respondent reported, "the program helped us spread awareness of our work and invite additional participation. One participant came back for an additional dialogue, bringing and interpreting for her husband. Later, her cousin called to ask to be included in the next dialogue." Overall, 99 percent of visitors said they would recommend the facilitated dialogue program they attended to others.[34]

The "America Is a Nation of Immigrants" Narrative Does Not Work

As early as 2008, network members began surveying their visitors on their visitors' interests and concerns around immigration past and present. Visitors to multiple network sites were also surveyed in 2009 and completed evaluations regarding their experience participating in immigration dialogues throughout the 2011 to 2013 training and program pilot phase. Results suggest that the "we are a nation of immigrants" model of immigration history, though spouted by visitors and many museums, is not always an effective model for opening dialogue across racial and ethnic difference. While this narrative provides a sense of shared identity based on immigration with the goal of showing that recent newcomers "aren't so different after all," unintentionally this framing reinforces divides among some audiences.

One concern expressed by visitors, museum staff, and advising scholars is that by continuing to affirm that America is a nation of immigrants, sites often unintentionally imply that the immigration process has changed little throughout the nation's history and that all who are interested in coming to the United States have had and continue to have equal access. As one visitor wrote, "A lot of my students, and by extension their parents, argue about legality or illegality of immigration, not realizing that this is a fairly new concept."[35] By contrast, sites like the Angel Island Immigration Station, which explicitly references the evolution of immigration policy up to and including today's immigration reform efforts, were more successful in avoiding an oversimplification of the experiences of contemporary immigrants.

This narrative also proved unsuccessful for other reasons, including visitors' tendency to romanticize the experience of their immigrant ancestors. While many visitors to the Lower East Side Tenement Museum and the Ellis Island Immigration Museum embraced their own ancestors' immigration stories and celebrated how immigration had built the nation in the past, many rejected parallels between those immigrants and people arriving today. For example, some asserted that immigrants arriving today drain more resources than they contribute, like the visitor who wrote on a Tenement Museum survey, "people today are coming for the wrong type of help. They come and abuse the system to their advantage and do not better themselves or their family." This desire to separate themselves from current immigrants was reflected in other regions of the country as well. One Southeastern site wrote, "We learned that in our community, European immigrants do not want to be considered immigrants in the contemporary context."[36]

This perspective proved particularly problematic in the American Southeast and Southwest, regions with large communities that are excluded from the "nation of immigrants" identity, such as African Americans and Native Americans. Interpretation that begins from this narrative as well as programs that ask participants to share "their immigrant story" left these audiences no place to engage in the immigration debate. Additionally, Southeastern communities, predominantly those with relatively recent immigrant populations, cited no public memory of immigration to draw from in confronting immigration today making this narrative ineffectual in promoting human connection.[37] Finally, many visitors across geographic regions felt that this was an exceptional historical moment in which national security concerns might require Americans to take a different approach to immigration than has been taken in the past.

How could these museums build on their historical assets to stimulate visitor understanding of immigration history, bridge divides across immigrant and receiving communities, and promote open and effective communication? Rather than describing America as a "nation of immigrants," a "melting pot," or a "patchwork quilt" and asking visitors to share their "immigrant story"—an all too common approach that shuts down contributions from visitors who do not embrace an "immigrant identity"—museums in the Immigration and Civil Rights Network utilized broader themes of interpretation that allowed for multiple entry points into these often sensitive conversations. Based on visitor survey results as well as findings from pilot dialogues, scholars, sites, and dialogue experts, four core themes have been identified that are successful in using historic immigration as a frame for engagement with contemporary immigration questions: Defining "We": Citizenship and American Identity; Defining Our Process: Restrictions and Legality; Defining Our Land: Borders and Freedom of Movement; and Defining Who We Protect: Civil Rights and Civil Liberties.

Defining "We": Citizenship and American Identity

Network sites continue to emphasize the importance of understanding how immigrant communities identify or are identified in relation to national borders—as is reflected, for example, in distinctions and debates about terminologies like Mexican/Hispanos/Tejano. Museums, like the National Hispanic Cultural Center (Albuquerque, New Mexico), explore evolving definitions of immigrant communities across constructs such as geography or time through examinations of the history, literature, and art of these communities. Their immigration dialogue program, *(Ex)change*, explores the immigrant experience within New Mexico and, more broadly, over the three-thousand-year Hispano experience. The program "builds on Mundos de Mestizaje, a 4000 square foot mural that presents the stories of powerful agents of history as well as the stories of everyday men, women, and children who have shaped Hispanic identity and cultural exchange [Mundos is Spanish for 'worlds'; Mestizaje refers to the hybrid nature of cultural identity]."[38] There is no real timeline to the content of the fresco though the work is embedded with images that explore the historical connections among arts, sciences, language, migration, and conflict working to affect the viewers' conceptions of change, exchange, and ultimately individual identity.

Facilitators of the *Ex(change)* dialogue program ask participants to examine how the mural constructs images of identity in the American Southwest. They then ask participants to list five adjectives that describe the person they are: in other words, "how do you identify yourself?" Afterward, facilitators ask participants to list five words that describe an American and facilitate conversation on the differences and similarities of their lists. As the dialogue continues, the facilitator shares a video of Sebastien de la Cruz, an eleven-year-old boy who sang the national anthem during game four of the 2013 National Basketball Association finals. His performance led to a national debate about whether this young man, a Mexican American who sang while wearing a traditional mariachi costume, should have been invited to perform. Facilitators then utilize an arc of dialogue to examine the following:

- Immigrants and their descendants in any country must balance being "American" with a desire to preserve their culture of origin. In your view, is one preferable to the other?

- Is this only an immigrant issue?

- Are there Americans, born and raised, who deal with the same challenges of balancing their cultural heritages with their American identities? Have you personally ever felt this to be a challenge?

Defining Our Process: Restrictions and Admittance

So much of today's immigration debate is defined by state and federal policy and the division between those who have entered the country through approved channels and those who have entered as "undocumented" immigrants. Some museums within the network, notably those based in historic immigration stations like the Ellis Island Immigration Station or those who interpret life along the border of the contemporary United States like Museo Urbano (El Paso, Texas), are uniquely equipped to discuss the history of immigrant admittance. Dialogue programs at these sites do not simply discuss the history of immigration policy, such as the passing of the Immigration Act of 1891, which moved the Bureau of Immigration under the Treasury Department and added new categories of restriction, excluding those with contagious diseases, polygamists, and contracted laborers. Rather, they work to redirect participant dialogue to a deeper discussion of how and why these policies came into effect and why they have changed throughout history. Moreover, these programs explicitly ask visitors to examine what today's policies say about our collective social values and personal beliefs about what values should drive American immigration policy. For example, a site discussing the Immigration Act of 1891 might encourage its visitors to explore the nation's stance toward admitting immigrants with a contagious disease today: Should the nation admit immigrants with HIV+ status? Should the nation actively welcome refugees from Ebola-afflicted nations like Sierra Leone? Should we quarantine American citizens, refugees, or newly arriving immigrants from Ebola-afflicted nations?

An example of an admittance policy–based dialogue program is one offered by the Angel Island Immigration Station Foundation, a site that tells the story of immigration after the 1924 Chinese Exclusion Act through a wealth of primary source documentation including immigration documents, photos, and the very walls of the site itself, which are inscribed with the poetry of immigrants who were detained there. Within their facilitated dialogue program, fourth graders critically examine the language of the 1924 law and discuss whether policies that excluded immigrants based on their race or ethnic identity were at heart "fair." They discuss when in their lives they have felt they were treated unfairly and how it affected them. Students choose poems carved into the walls of the detainees' dormitory that resonate for them and use the poems as the basis by which to answer arc of dialogue questions such as:

- How would you feel if you were excluded or left out based on your appearance?

- When the Angel Island Immigration Station was in operation, the federal government made decisions based on race, who was healthy, who had money, who could read and write in their own language, and so forth. Are these reasons fair?

- What reason do you think would be better? Or should anyone be let into the country?

- What can you do when you know someone is being treated unfairly?

Defining Our Land: Borders and Freedom of Movement

Popular understanding of immigration often characterizes it as a one-way process, from one country of origin to one country of destination, ending in assimilation. However, historians have long acknowledged that migratory paths among many groups past and present are often back and forth or circular, resulting in new global identities.[39] The Arab American National Museum (Dearborn, Michigan) asks its visitors to consider that the frequency and distance by which we travel has fostered global identities that may or may not align with our contemporary understandings of assimilation through questions like: Who is an American citizen? Who is a global citizen? Should our nation support dual citizenship? And can you be patriotic to more than one nation?

Additionally, this theme asks visitors to explore not only the physical boundaries that create a nation, but the social and emotional as well. How does one individual's right to feel safe intersect with my right to go where I need to go to feel safe? The Museo Urbano *Border Immigration Dialogues* provide university students, many of whom have personal experiences with immigration, and other community members an opportunity to reflect in a place that historically has been, and is still, shaped by immigration. Museo Urbano takes the stance that the entire two-thousand-mile border between the United States and

Mexico is a site of conscience. They believe that "the border is a place where communities and individuals experience social, political and economic struggles on a daily basis. It is also a place that reflects a long history of conquest, labor exploitation, denial of basic human rights and other tragedies. It is a place where generations have struggled for human rights. It is a unique site of memory, inspiration, vision, and creativity."[40]

Defining Who We Protect: Civil Rights and Civil Liberties

Much of the immigration history told at museums and historic sites in the United States is centered on the experience of immigrants in longstanding urban centers on the coasts and borderlands. But the Southeastern United States is home to the newest and fastest-growing immigrant population in the country. This recent demographic shift has both challenged and retrenched old precepts. Facilitated dialogue programs working with this theme aim to open connections between the experiences of immigrant, refugee, and African American communities by highlighting the historical connection between the civil rights movement in the United States and the international movements for human rights. In their dialogue series *Immigration as a 21st Century Human Rights Issue*, the National Center for Civil and Human Rights (Atlanta, Georgia) explores how communities move from stereotypes and fear toward inclusion and acceptance. Through films, artistic performances, and conversations led by academics and civil and human rights leaders, the center "will draw on the rich history of Atlanta as the think tank of the Civil Rights Movement, and address how the tools and strategies of that movement can be used to foster the change sought in order to create a welcoming community."[41] The facilitated dialogue program targets family groups, youth groups, and gender-specific groups as a cross-section of the Atlanta community.

Branding Immigration Dialogue Programs Correctly Is Vital to a Program's Success

From the beginning of their involvement in the Immigration and Civil Rights Network, sites were ever aware that although they were working together as a peer-driven nationally based collaborative, the regional contexts they were working in were vastly different. In the Southeast, civil rights museums were working in historically black/white communities recently transformed by immigration. In the Northeast, a region with long histories and strong public memories of immigration, museums reported tensions among visitors eager to establish that their ancestors were different from today's immigrants. Museums in the Southwest and along the West Coast struggled to complicate the prevailing attitude among visitors that immigration was only a "Latino issue." Recognizing and working with these regional differences was vital in developing successful marketing strategies for the sites' dialogue offerings.

Many sites in the Southeast found that "immigration" was a highly polarizing term and that using it within the name of a program or within the program's description limited overall program attendance: "We learned concretely that using the term immigrant or immigration was a turn off to many, especially in a highly charged election year and as the city [Charlotte, North Carolina] hosted the Democratic National Convention. Examining immigration as an example of demographic shifts from a black and white South to a more diverse community was intriguing to people—but, not a dialogue around immigration."[42]

Throughout the Southwest, sites like the Arizona State Museum (Tucson, Arizona) found higher success in attracting visitors when they branded programs not as "immigration" programs but instead used words such as "journey" or "movement," which allowed for Native American populations to find their ways into a topic that had previously been exclusionary. "Immigration" was also polarizing for staff at the Bob Bullock Texas State History Museum (Austin, Texas). The museum is just over three hundred miles from the US–Mexico border and recognizes immigration as a key part of the state's history. However, talking about contemporary immigration issues in a state-owned museum is difficult as the staff, board members, and ultimately the state government work to avoid the perception of political agendas. Similarly, attracting an audience to discuss such issues in their leisure time seemed unlikely to staff members familiar with repeat visitors of the museum. Thus, staff purposely avoided use of the word "immigration" and instead developed marketing language and a programmatic focus on the question of "Who is a Texan?" Within the program, participants take a tour of the museum's core exhibition and engage in facilitated dialogue exploring how they define themselves, how they became a Texas resident, what "Texan identity" means to them, and whether immigration is strengthening or erasing the Texan identity.

Facilitated Dialogue on Contentious Social Issues Isn't Easy

Addressing contentious community issues through facilitated dialogue programs is draining work. Participants drawn to these programs are often passionate, socially engaged people who feel strongly about their personal experiences and perspectives. Placing these audience members in dialogue with those whose beliefs may be in direct opposition to their own requires museum staff to invest in their work in a new way. The move from interpreter or educator to facilitator is not an easy one and asks staff to give of themselves personally, releasing control over a museum-goer's experience in an effort to move conversations forward toward personal and collective growth.

In an era in which funders are increasingly less enthusiastic about investing in professional gatherings, evaluation after evaluation made the case that if museums are at heart communal spaces and if we want to change institutions of passive learning into institutions of active engagement, then we must train our professionals in the manner in which we are asking them to engage. This is "in-person" work and it requires "in-person" training so as to best model new communication techniques effectively.

In-person training also serves the added benefit of helping to create a strong peer-led network, which has proven key to supporting the needs of each site's new facilitators. Over the course of the past six years, participants consistently ranked the opportunity to speak with and learn from their colleagues as vital to their own professional growth. Said one participant, "There are so many things I valued about this. I loved spending time with other professionals who share the same interests of wanting to expand the possibilities of museum education and programming through an inclusive and sensitive mindset."[43] Overwhelmingly, site representatives cited the opportunity to experience facilitated dialogue programs on site at their colleagues' institutions as "inspirational." When asked what about the Immigration and Civil Rights Network was most valuable to her, Dr. Yolanda Leyva from Museo Urbano wrote, "Finding my people. I feel less alone in my field and in my work because I am now connected with others who share my values about public history, history and activism, museums as community organizations and educating people about human rights issues."[44]

Since their initial gathering in 2008, the Immigration and Civil Rights Network has grown to over thirty-five members who define themselves as new forums for dialogue across difference on the most challenging immigration issues our communities face. Sites represent a variety of immigrant and ethnic histories and are spread across the United States in urban, suburban, Midwestern, and borderland communities. The network includes sites like the Museum of International Folk Art (Santa Fe, New Mexico) that uses art as a common medium through which to engage visitors in facilitated dialogue around constantly evolving definitions of "home" and the Museum of Tolerance (Los Angeles, California) that has reenvisioned elementary school programming for one of its core exhibitions, *Finding Our Families, Finding Ourselves*, to use dialogic methodology with the hope of promoting a more nuanced understanding of American diversity.

The network includes museums of ethnic identity, sites of American immigration history, and museums like the Atlanta History Center (Atlanta, Georgia), located in a region experiencing unprecedented and recent demographic shifts, that is asking Southeastern communities to redefine their commonly accepted identities as historic black/white communities in order to reflect an increasingly diverse population. At least six members of the network define themselves as civil rights museums that have made a new commitment to developing exhibitions and programs that connect the experiences of African Americans and immigrants.

The National Dialogues on Immigration Project was a manifestation of the network's ongoing commitment to making history relevant to today's audiences and actively modeled how museums might use facilitated dialogue as a tool to accomplish this. Their approach, refined over the course of six years, may prove vital in helping communities grapple with the ongoing challenges and benefits of contemporary immigration. Speaking of the National Dialogues on Immigration Project, Dr. David Goldfield, PhD, professor of history at the University of North Carolina, Charlotte, said,

> The dialogues highlight the unique and shared experiences of diverse ethnic and racial groups . . . and the nation as a whole. The dialogues reflect the distinctive process of how each of these groups adjusted to American society and how that society changed as a result. . . . As the United States becomes a more multi-racial society, as it has become a multi-ethnic society, these dialogues facilitate the acceptance of multiple identities as part of a broader historical process that has shaped the nation since its founding.[45]

Their work is important because today, in spite of the fact that recent polls show that the majority of Americans support a pathway to citizenship for the 11.1 million undocumented immigrants living in the United States, state lawmakers have sought to enact legislation that would result in increased scrutiny of immigrants by law enforcement and would limit educational access and criminalize citizen interaction with undocumented immigrants.[46] While nearly two-thirds of voters in rural communities say immigration is good for America, seven out of ten support highly restrictive immigration laws, laws that may make it more difficult for immigrants to legally enter the country. The disconnect is striking. If immigration is good for the nation, why make it more difficult for people to come here? Or is immigration actually not good for America? In their commitment to be nonprescriptive, museums like those involved in the National Dialogues on Immigration Project do not attempt to sway visitor opinion in either direction. Instead, they share a common resolve to share historical perspectives, encourage personal and collective learning, and help communities resolve such disconnects for themselves by making opportunities for open dialogue accessible in every community across America.

Notes

1. Sarah Edkins, "National Dialogues on Immigration 2014," *International Coalition of Sites of Conscience Publicity Brief*, 2013.

2. International Coalition of Sites of Conscience, "Immigration Sites of Conscience Needs Assessment," August 2008.

3. International Coalition of Sites of Conscience, "Network Descriptions," accessed December 18, 2014, http://www.sitesofconscience.org/networks/asia/.

4. John Chesser, "Charlotte's Rapid Growth Brings Demographic Changes," UNC Charlotte Urban Institute, February 11, 2011, accessed February 10, 2014, http://ui.uncc.edu/story/charlottes-rapid-growth-brings-demographic-changes.

5. Jeffrey S. Passel and D'Vera Cohn, "Unauthorized Immigrants: 11.1 Million in 2001," *Pew Hispanic Center*, December 6, 2012, accessed February 10, 2014, http://www.pewhispanic.org/2012/12/06/unauthorized-immigrants-11-1-million-in-2011/.

6. Brentin Mock, "Hate Crimes against Latinos Rising Nationwide," *Southern Poverty Law Center Intelligence Report* 128 (Winter 2007).

7. International Coalition of Sites of Conscience, "Immigration Sites of Conscience Network Seminar Report," August 2008.

8. International Coalition of Sites of Conscience, "Minutes of the Immigration Sites of Conscience Network Meeting," August 8–13, 2008.

9. Ibid.

10. International Coalition of Sites of Conscience, "Seminar Report."

11. Tammy Bormann, "Facilitated Dialogue: Methodology and Applications," training presented at a meeting of the International Coalition of Sites of Conscience, Sleepy Hollow, New York, August 9, 2008.

12. Barbara Schaffer Bacon, Cheryl Yuen, and Pam Korza, *Animating Democracy: The Artistic Imagination as a Force in Civic Dialogue: A Report Commissioned by the Ford Foundation* (Washington, DC: Americans for the Arts, 1999).

13. United States Census Bureau, "2000 Census," accessed February 9, 2014, http://www.census.gov/2000census/data/.

14. Lowell National Historic Park Staff, "Moving Conversations Program Model Draft," January 2014.

15. Ibid.

16. International Coalition of Sites of Conscience, "Seminar Report."

17. Ibid.

18. International Coalition of Sites of Conscience, "Civil Rights Sites of Conscience Workshop Report," July 2009.

19. International Coalition of Sites of Conscience, "Minutes of the Civil Rights Sites of Conscience Workshop," June 25–28, 2009.

20. Ibid.

21. Isabel Rubio, email to Erika Gee, August 20, 2009.

22. International Coalition of Sites of Conscience, "Formative Evaluation Survey on Contemporary Immigration," February 2011.

23. Ibid.

24. International Coalition of Sites of Conscience, "NEH Planning Team Meeting Agenda," February 2011.

25. International Coalition of Sites of Conscience, "Immigration Sites of Conscience Regional Training Project," application to the Institute of Museum and Library Services, August 2010.

26. International Coalition of Sites of Conscience, "NEH Planning Team Meeting Minutes," February 2011.

27. Conny Graft, "2013 Evaluation Report for the International Coalition of Sites of Conscience National Dialogues on Immigration Project," December 2013.

28. International Coalition of Sites of Conscience, "Evaluation Survey," 2011.

29. T. F. Pettigrew and L. R. Tropp, "A Meta-Analytic Test of Intergroup Contact Theory," *Journal of Personality and Social Psychology* 90 (2006): 751–83.

30. Graft, "Evaluation Report."

31. Roy Rosenzweig and David Thelen, *The Presence of the Past* (New York: Columbia University Press, 1998), 91–105.

32. Graft, "Evaluation Report."

33. Ibid.

34. Ibid.

35. Ibid.

36. Ibid.

37. International Coalition of Sites of Conscience, "National Dialogues on Immigration Project," application to the National Endowment for the Humanities, August 2012.

38. Erica Garcia, "Dialogue Program Model Description, National Hispanic Cultural Center," January 2014.

39. Donna Gabaccia and Vicki Ruiz, *American Dreaming, Global Realities: Rethinking U.S. Immigration History* (Chicago: University of Illinois Press, 2006).

40. Yolanda Leyva, "Dialogue Program Model Description, Museo Urbano," January 2014.

41. Deborah Richardson, "Dialogue Program Model Description, National Center for Civil and Human Rights," January 2014.

42. Graft, "Evaluation Report."

43. Ibid.

44. Ibid.

45. David Goldfield, "National Dialogues on Immigration Project," support letter accompanying application to the National Endowment for the Humanities, August 2012.

46. A post–2012 presidential election poll conducted by *ABC News* and the *Washington Post* showed 57 percent of Americans stated that they support a pathway for citizenship for undocumented immigrants, and in exit polling completed on election day close to two-thirds of all Americans, 65 percent, said undocumented immigrants in the United States should be "offered a chance to apply for legal status."

CHAPTER ONE

THE ARAB AMERICAN
NATIONAL MUSEUM

Anan Ameri

Introduction

In May 2005, we celebrated the inauguration of the Arab American National Museum (AANM), the first and only institution in the United States dedicated to telling the story of Arab Americans. The AANM, a project of ACCESS,[1] is a 38,500-square-foot educational and cultural institution located in the heart of Dearborn, Michigan, home to a large number of Arab Americans, many of whom are recent immigrants (photo 1.1). The location of the museum, across the street from Dearborn City Hall,[2] a city that had been historically hostile to ethnic and racial minorities, is a testimony to the determination and perseverance of this community. The AANM's mission is to "document, preserve and present the history, culture and contributions of Arab Americans." It joins other ethnic museums in providing the public with a better understanding and appreciation of the diversity of our nation.

Arab Americans have been an integral part of United States history since the country's inception. The number of Arab Americans grew substantially during the era of mass immigration from 1880 to 1924. Early immigrants worked as peddlers, grocers, and unskilled workers. After World War I, Arab Americans were attracted to Metro Detroit because of its booming automobile industry, especially Henry Ford's eight-hour, five-dollar work day. Many Arab Americans settled in Dearborn at the foot of the Ford's Rouge Plant. Later, they continued to arrive, even in times of economic recession, attracted to the security provided by extended family and fellow villagers who had already settled in the area. Today, Arab immigrants, as well as Arab Americans from other states, are drawn to Metro Detroit by a sense of belonging provided by the size and diversity of the community and its well-established educational, religious, and cultural institutions. In spite of their long presence and significant contributions, Arab Americans (as is the case with many minorities) have been subjected to negative stereotyping and vilification, which increased dramatically in the wake of September 11. The fact that a substantial

Photo 1.1.   The AANM courtyard.
Arab American National Museum.

number of recent Arab immigrants are also Muslim has exasperated the hostility toward them.

While the official date of inaugurating the AANM is May 5, 2005, ACCESS established its Cultural Arts Program,[3] which later matured into the museum, as early as 1987. The primary strength of the Cultural Arts Program, and later the museum, has been its ability to respond to the demographic changes in both the Arab American community as well as the community at large. The growing number of new immigrants has created a thriving diversity in the area and has influenced the AANM exhibitions and public programming as well as its relationships with non-Arab cultural and community-based organizations. Most importantly, it has allowed us to live up to our core values as stated in all the AANM strategic plans: "Our core values embody our belief that the cultural heritage of all people ought to be preserved, celebrated, and shared with others. We value the arts not only as an aesthetic expression of our human experience, but also as a powerful tool that empowers people, instills community pride, and bridges some of the racial, ethnic, and global divisions that have separated communities and nations for too long."

Possibly the most unique and valuable aspect of the Arab American National Museum is that it occurs in the context of a broader organization (ACCESS) that has worked for the empowerment of the Arab American community and *all* communities of color for almost forty-five years. These values of empowerment, inclusivity, and respect for diversity fueled collaborative relationships with other ethnic minorities. True, the AANM is an ethnically specific institution; however, we never envisioned ourselves to be exclusive. On the contrary, we continuously strive to be responsive and reflective of our nation's demographic changes, to dispel many of the misconceptions about Arab Americans and other minorities, and to help all ethnic groups recognize their shared histories, experiences, and interdependence. In fact, one of the AANM's stated values is to be inclusive by "bridging communities through high-quality and compelling arts and cultural programming."

Consequently, the AANM has been playing a leading role in bringing various racial and ethnic communities to collaborate together. Most notable of this work is the Cultural Exchange Network, a coalition of almost fifty ethnic and immigrant communities that work together to produce the annual "Forum on Race, Ethnicity and Culture and the Concert of Colors," an annual four-day, highly visible community-building event that celebrates the diversity of our region through musical, artistic, and spoken word performances.

The AANM exhibitions are also strategic and respond to the needs and concerns of the Arab American community. *Women in Time of War* (2006) was our response to the war in Iraq and the tendency of the media and politicians to glorify wars rather than focus on their horrors and civilian casualties, especially among women and children. *Connecting Communities* (2009), to be discussed later in more detail, deals with the continued attacks on immigrant communities. *Patriots and Peace Makers: Arab Americans in Service to Our Nation* (2011) was a response to the relentless and continued attacks on Arab Americans' patriotism and their portrayal as nontrustworthy. Finally, *Little Syria* (2013) was in response to the vicious reaction to the idea of expanding an already existing mosque in Lower Manhattan, close to the World Trade Center, an area that was historically an Arab American neighborhood known as Little Syria (photo 1.2). In 2016, we opened *What We Carried: Fragments & Memories from Iraq & Syria*, which tells the refugee experience through the objects that they brought with them (photo 1.3). This exhibit is currently traveling the country.

The AANM is one of the many ethnic and civil rights museums that have been created in the last few decades; other examples include the Japanese American National Museum in Los Angeles, the Wing Luke Museum in Seattle, the National Museum of the American Indian in Washington, DC, and the National Underground Railroad Freedom Center in Cincinnati. The creation of these museums was (for the most part) a response to the exclusion of minorities and their perspectives from mainstream museums. These ethnically specific museums have been playing leading roles in providing more accurate and comprehensive narratives of our nation's history. Their inclusive approaches have given voice to those who had been historically marginalized because of race, class, ethnicity, or time of immigration. By doing so, they have been challenging mainstream museums to become more involved in issues that are of concern to the communities they claim to serve. Institutions such as these are destined to reshape our understanding and widen our horizons in terms of what defines the arts, aesthetics, and culture, and, more importantly, they will help us better define concepts such as cultural advocacy, representation, community, and audience participation.

Photo 1.2. AANM *Little Syria* traveling exhibit opening in New York, May 2017.
Arab American National Museum.

Photo 1.3. AANM *Little Syria* exhibit.
Arab American National Museum.

The AANM Participatory Approach

From the early onset of AANM planning in 1999, we were challenged with creating a balance between being simultaneously a "professional" and a progressive grassroots institution that is rooted in its community. Since our inception as a museum, we have called upon members of local and national Arab American communities to become stewards of their own history and to incorporate their voices in the permanent exhibitions. We have reached out to these communities to *lead* the process of determining which artifacts, archival materials, and personal narratives are significant to them and which reflect the overall community's diversity, experiences, and contributions. For more than eight months in 2002, the museum's founding executive staff traveled around the country and held meetings and focus groups in cities that have large Arab American populations. We posed questions about what they would like to see in an Arab American museum and what would successfully show how the museum reflects the community's diverse experiences.

From these meetings, it was clear that people wanted the museum to both reflect the beauty and richness of Arab architecture and to be modern at the same time, to have a section about the contributions of the Arab diaspora to the world's civilizations, and to address the issue of stereotyping and the exclusion of Arab Americans from history books and cultural institutions. They wanted the museum's exhibitions to reflect the diversity, work, contributions, and long presence of Arabs in the United States. Many focus participants mentioned the fact that Arab Americans have been part of the fabric of the United States since its inception and have fought and died for this country since the War of Independence. These messages were critical in shaping the building, exhibitions, and public programming of the museum.

The role of museums in engaging their communities and becoming a space for conversations about important issues is being recognized more and more nationally and internationally. Gabriela Aidar focuses her work on community members whom she refers to as "non-audiences"; that is, people who are typically marginalized by museums and who are often excluded from museums' cultural offerings. During a presentation at the 2011 Salzburg Global Seminar titled "Communities and Culture," she made several important points about the participatory culture of museums. Among these points was that "museums create social narratives and these narratives can be used to include or to marginalize as well as to legitimatize or eradicate prejudice."[4] She added the following:

> How can Museums and libraries use their strength to reflect demographic and cultural shifts? By how they select the stories they tell and the resources they offer. If libraries and museums intentionally use their resources to reflect and create change in societies, they must first be institutionally committed to the idea that Museums can and must collaborate to strengthen cultural diversity.[5]

These points resonate with the AANM's mission, vision, and values. From the beginning, the AANM has tackled the question of how to engage and collectively represent the national Arab American community in its exhibitions and programming. We have taken risks in approaching exhibitions in nonconventional ways by involving our local and national communities, with their diversity and multiple perspectives, in all that we do. This approach has served us well and has helped us connect with Arab American communities locally and nationally and has helped us establish ourselves as a leader in strengthening and bringing these very diverse communities together.

There are multiple discussions about the value of this approach across the field. In her article "Coming to the Center of Community Life," Maria-Rosario Jackson suggests that museums should be challenged to "stretch their boundaries, step away from the sidelines, come to the center of civic life, and become a more active participant and even a leader in social capital and the community building process."[6] This is further reinforced by people in the field who are examining the role of historical societies in preserving and interpreting history, as Barbara Franco writes:

> Rather than viewing themselves as elite or scholarly experts who take responsibility for telling the community's history, historical societies increasingly see themselves as facilitators who are helping various communities within the city tell their stories. This approach not only reflects a general trend toward multiculturalism within the academic community, it is also indicative of a new emphasis on public relations. . . . A strong relationship with the local community is essential to this equation.[7]

The AANM has continued to redefine its relationship with the Arab American community during each stage of its development. This process has enabled us to incorporate the national community in our program development while conditioning our ability to respond to its changing and evolving needs. We continue refining this participatory model that engenders a bilateral relationship between museums and communities rather than encouraging the unilateral relationship that has typically defined traditional museum practices.[8] In each of our projects, we call on members of the Arab American community and other ethnic communities to become stewards of their own histories and to *lead* the process of determining which artifacts, materials, and personal narratives are significant to them. By engaging our communities in this deliberate and thoughtful process we have been able to develop a truly collaborative model that can be replicated by others across the museum field. We believe that this model has great potential to redefine the dynamic between institutions and communities and will create an environment in which the role of the museum is truly transformed, making it much more responsive and valuable to its communities.

Further, we believe that a rise in participatory expectations among museums across the country, and around the world for that matter, will only offer greater and more creative opportunities for sustained community engagement and "people-led" projects that value the museum not as a static place, but as one that is dynamic, accessible, and personally meaningful. Speaking to this, museum scholar Dr. Serhan Ada of Istanbul's Bilgi University has written that "participation occurs when someone welcomed as a guest feels as though they have become a host."[9]

Connecting Communities

Since the 1970s our nation, including Southeast Michigan, has been witnessing a major demographic change due to the influx of a large number of immigrants from different parts of the world. As this trend continues and the number of foreign-born Americans increases, it is anticipated that European Americans will become a minority by 2042. This drastic shift in the ethnic and racial composition of our nation's population has been an unwelcome change in many communities that have not previously encountered immigrants living in their midst. Today, immigration policy and immigrant status continue to be contentious subjects of national public debate. Immigrants are often portrayed as a threat to the "American" way of life and a burden on "our" economy. Stereotypes and misconceptions about immigrants in the region abound and public opinion about immigration is often tainted by this debate. Additionally, the "immigration issue" has become a lightning rod in today's media coverage and in political debates, especially since 9/11 and more recent economic meltdowns. The current level of controversy makes it almost impossible to have civil and rational discussions about immigration, even as our economy recovers. Rarely do people, especially immigrants, have an opportunity to get directly involved in discussing these important issues or to interact directly with communities other than their own. Furthermore, and partly because of this hostility, immigrant communities often live in their own enclaves and feel intimidated and excluded from this national debate. Believing in the role of museums as proactive institutions and centers for civic engagement and civil dialogue, the AANM decided to tackle the issue of immigration directly by creating a new exhibition titled *Connecting Communities*. While Michigan had not attracted immigrants in the same numbers it did in the past, Metro Detroit continues to be home to multiple immigrant communities. *Connecting Communities* focuses on three neighborhoods: Dearborn, which has a large number of recent Arab American immigrants; Southwest Detroit, with its large Hispanic population; and Hamtramck, which is home to multiple immigrant communities including Yemenis, Southeast Asians, and Eastern Europeans. During the late 1990s and early 2000s, Detroit and its adjacent suburbs were suffering from declining populations and deteriorating services at a time when these three neighborhoods were thriving and enjoying increasing populations, growing economies, and high employment. Immigrants were purchasing and renovating boarded up buildings, including the building where the Arab American National Museum stands today, and opening new family businesses. These communities have their own ethnic food stores, restaurants, and places of worship. Most importantly, they have established their own social service agencies to meet the needs of their communities. In spite of this reality, anti-immigrant sentiments were as strong in Michigan as they were, and continue to be, around the country.

Connecting Communities brought together twenty university students, community leaders, immigrants, and their organizations to tackle this very timely and relevant issue. It provided immigrants from the previously mentioned neighborhoods the opportunity to tell their stories and narrate their own experiences. It provided college students from various immigrant and nonimmigrant communities the opportunity to be directly involved in

Photo 1.4. AANM *Connecting Communities* exhibit.
Arab American National Museum.

the national and local discussion about immigration. Furthermore, the project was intentionally designed to foster intergenerational interaction as students met and interviewed older people, heard and recorded their stories, and collected their artifacts, photographs, and historical documents. *Connecting Communities* culminated in a temporary exhibition at the AANM (October 1, 2009 to March 28, 2010). The exhibition, coupled with guided tours and public programming, helped our audiences learn about the diversity of our area and helped them gain better understanding of immigrants and our nation's history of immigration (photo 1.4). It is worth noting that after later traveling to a few locations in Michigan, the exhibition found its permanent home at the Garage Cultural Center of Art and Creativity, a Latin American cultural organization in Detroit.

Project Design

Connecting Communities is a multicomponent project composed of the following: (1) a series of classes for students that gave them a better understanding about the history of immigration and that equipped them to conduct interviews and collect oral histories; (2) fieldwork through which students identified and interviewed community members and collected artifacts, photographs, and historical documents; (3) a traveling exhibition that students were involved in creating; and (4) a series of public programming that included but was not limited to a series of cultural performances from the various communities represented in the exhibition, a panel discussion by students and immigrants, a series of lectures and films, and guided tours of small groups (ten to fifteen people) that included a pre- and post-tour dialogue about the exhibition and the issue of immigration. Prior to starting the project, the AANM contacted university professors in the Detroit area to solicit their support in recruiting some of their students and to give the students one semester's work of class credit for their efforts to develop the project. Additionally, the museum offered the students an hourly stipend for their work.

Class Series

The first component was a series of six classes that met once a week and used a curriculum guide and syllabus created by the museum staff and scholars made specifically for this project. These scholars also participated as instructors in the class series, which included the following:

- a guided tour of the museum's permanent exhibits (emphasizing the history of Arab immigration and tangible examples of the use of individual stories, artifacts, and photographs in historical documentation)

- an overview of our nation's immigration history (with special emphasis on Michigan's and Metro Detroit's immigration history)

- the role of material culture and oral narratives in preserving history

- training in oral history and artifact collection methods

- a field trip to the *Dearborn Press and Guide* newspaper (where students learned more about interview techniques)

- identifying themes relevant to the issue of immigration (to be used during the students' field work)

Documentation/Field Work

Using their selected themes and drawing on what they had learned during their course work, students (in teams of two) interviewed and collected oral histories and artifacts from immigrants in one of the previously mentioned neighborhoods. A professional photojournalist accompanied each of the student teams and visually documented the people being interviewed, their families, and their communities. These photographs, along with the oral histories, artifacts, and other important documents collected by the students, captured a specific moment in the development of these immigrant communities. AANM staff, along with the humanities scholars, worked with the students to help them with their interviews and artifact collection.

Exhibit Production

During this stage, students worked with the AANM curatorial staff and the humanities scholars to decide on the exhibition's themes, choose the photos, artifacts, and clippings from their oral histories, and determine the layout and design for the final product. A local exhibition design firm and the AANM curatorial staff handled the fabrication of the exhibit.

The *Connecting Communities* exhibition opened to the public on March 1, 2009. The opening featured a public reception that included the participating students and their families, the interviewees and their families, and members and organizations from various immigrant communities. The opening also included a symposium that addressed the contribution of immigrants to Metro Detroit, a reflection on the experience from the perspective of participating students and interviewees, and the common concerns and shared experiences of various immigrant communities. The public programming that accompanied the exhibition allowed for a public discussion about immigration and provided a safe space for immigrants to interact with our visitors and share their views and experiences.

The Exhibition

The *Connecting Communities* exhibition, like other AANM projects, was entirely community-based. The diversity of those featured in the exhibition mimicked the diversity of AANM visitors and the local community. It highlighted the three mentioned neighborhoods with special focus on nine immigrants whose photos were displayed on large, freestanding panels along with quotes from their oral histories. Immigrants vividly described their journeys to the United States and their ensuing struggles and victories. Several of the immigrants explained their reasons for immigrating through the context of larger issues in their countries of origin, such as war, economic struggle, or a lack of opportunities.

Many of the interviewees went on to describe their warm feelings toward their new adopted country and their hopes for a better life for themselves and their children. The exhibition's audio component allowed visitors to hear the immigrants tell their own stories. A display of personal artifacts and memorabilia were also included in the exhibition. Within the exhibition, several interactive tools encouraged participation and promoted dialogue among our visitors. For example, during its display at the AANM, a large US map was projected on one wall of the exhibition's gallery. Using this map and color-coded graphs, participants learned the history of immigration, the extent of immigration, and the geographic sources of immigration. They could track immigration to America by region, decade, and ethnic group. Another wall displayed an AANM-produced video depicting the local immigrant communities highlighted within the exhibition. An important component of the exhibition was a computer where visitors could create YouTube videos recording their own thoughts about immigration. YouTube was perhaps the best way to harness the reaction and impact of the exhibition on visitors. It allowed them to share an opinion or idea not only with their docents and group members but also with others via the internet. Taken together, all these exhibit features encouraged visitors to examine and share their views and attitudes regarding immigration.

Guided Tours

Using the dialogic model developed by the International Coalition of Sites of Conscience,[10] the museum's education department developed a special docent-guided tour.

Photo 1.5. AANM *Coming to America* permanent exhibit.
Arab American National Museum.

To connect past and present immigration, the tour included not only the *Connecting Communities* exhibition, but also the AANM *Coming to America* permanent exhibition. Within *Connecting Communities*, docents discussed the immigrants' stories and highlighted differences and similarities between them—why they immigrated, from where they immigrated, and the reasons why they chose to settle in the Detroit area. In the *Coming to America* exhibition, participants learned about the history of Arab American immigration starting as early as 1528, when the first enslaved Arab Moroccan arrived. The exhibition explored different waves of immigration and the extent to which Arab American immigration stories related to the larger immigration experience of all Americans (photo 1.5).

Before this special tour began, participants were engaged in a dialogue session designed to gauge their levels of understanding and perhaps bring to light any biases or preconceived notions they might have had about immigrants. After touring the exhibitions, participants were engaged in another dialogue session about what they learned and whether the exhibitions influenced their perceptions and understandings about immigration and immigrants. While the *Connecting Communities* exhibition was effective on its own, viewing it with a docent-guided tour and participating in pre- and post-dialogues vastly increased visitors' levels of understanding. It also helped staff members gain better insights into what, if any, changes occurred in our visitors' knowledge and attitudes and what aspects of the exhibition and tour they found most informative and engaging.

The tours and dialogues also helped us evaluate the extent to which we were effectively achieving the project's goals.

Conclusion

The impact of *Connecting Communities* goes far beyond the museum and its visitors. It is intended to instill a sense of pride and unity among various immigrant communities while serving as a model for other museums grappling with the issue of representation and participation. This project was based on the model developed by AANM when it created its original permanent exhibitions. During the planning phase of the AANM we were determined to have the permanent exhibitions reflect the complexity of the Arab American experience. Claiming that we need to tell the Arab American story using our own voice assumes that Arab Americans have one voice and one story, which of course is not true. The same principle applies to other immigrant communities that are not only extremely diverse in terms of their ethnicities, socioeconomic statuses, and religious backgrounds, but also in their personal experiences.

Through this participatory approach, significant emphasis is placed on having immigrant communities document their own experiences and learn the processes by which they can harness their own histories in lasting and permanent ways. The approach also addresses how museums can empower marginalized communities and support them in recognizing that they are an integral and important part of our nation and that their stories *are* the American story. *Connecting Communities* has also demonstrated a museum's role, or rather responsibility, in bringing communities together to collectively chip away at the prevailing misconceptions, myths, and stereotypes about immigrants and other minorities. It offers a model for how a museum's activities can extend beyond its walls and geographic location. It embodies a model that focuses on a process typically reserved for museum archivists and research teams, one that invites community members to collect artifacts, stories, and important documents that best represent their own histories, impacts, and contributions.

This participatory approach has also been very valuable to our staff. It has strengthened their knowledge about Arab Americans and non-Arab immigrant communities and has fostered a collaborative relationship between the AANM and other ethnic organizations and cultural institutions. The material that we have collected has not only been valuable in creating and enriching the AANM exhibitions and archives but has also been valuable to the fields of ethnic, American, and immigration studies as well as to anyone interested in learning more about immigration. Finally, this approach continues to allow us to emphasize the importance of involving communities in telling their own stories. It allows us to continue approaching our programs and exhibitions with a keen eye for "people-led" initiatives that are truly reflective of the community we strive to include and represent. Hopefully, it will contribute to redefining the role of museums as institutions that are truly inclusive of their communities and audiences. As we have developed and continue to develop our permanent and traveling exhibitions, it is important to always keep in mind Dr. Serhan Ada's comment that "participation occurs when someone welcomed as a guest feels as though they have become a host."[11]

Notes

1. ACCESS is an Arab American social service organization established in 1972 in response to the increased number of Arab immigrants as well as high unemployment, especially among autoworkers.

2. The Dearborn City Hall, a ninety-three-year-old historic building, was sold in 2013 to Artspace. In 2014 the city operation moved to a new Dearborn administrative center.

3. In May 2005, the Cultural Program was integrated into the Arab American National Museum upon the museum's opening.

4. Gabriela Aidar, "Culture and Communities," panel discussion presented at the Salzburg Global Seminar: Libraries and Museums in an Era of Participatory Culture, October 19–23, 2011. Information can also be found in *Libraries and Museums in an Era of Participatory Culture* (a partnership project of the Salzburg Global Seminar and the Institute of Museum and Library Services), Session 482 report, prepared by Deborah L. Mack, ed. Nancy Rogers and Susanna Seidl-Fox, accessed December 5, 2012, http://www.imls.gov/assets/1/AssetManager/SGS_Report_2012.pdf.

5. Ibid.

6. Maria-Rosario Jackson, "Coming to the Center of Community Life," in *Mastering Civic Engagement: A Challenge to Museums* (Washington, DC: American Association of Museums 2002), 29–30.

7. Barbara Franco, "In Urban History Museums and Historical Agencies," in *Public History: Essays from the Field*, ed. James B. Gardner and Peter S. LaPaglia (Malabar, FL: Krieger Publishing Company, 1999), 313.

8. Freda Nicholson and W. Richard West, "Forward," in *Mastering Civic Engagement: A Challenge to Museums* (Washington, DC: American Association of Museums, 2002), xxi. Authors Nicholson and West discuss the significance of community engagement and the transformative power that communities can have on museums when properly incorporated into their program development. This transformation is a redefinition in a sense of the museum itself, from becoming a place that is merely a presenting institution to a center that truly engages and represents its audiences in a participatory and meaningful way.

9. Rob Stein, "Is Your Community Better Off Because it has a Museum? Final Thoughts About Participatory Culture (Part III)," November 3, 2011, http://www.imamuseum.org/blog/2011/11/03/is-your-community-better-off-because-it-has-a-museum-final-thoughts-about-participatory-culture-part-iii/.

10. The AANM is a founding member of the International Coalition of Sites of Conscience.

11. Stein, "Is Your Community Better Off Because it has a Museum?"

SPEAKING OF CHANGE IN A NEW IMMIGRANT GATEWAY

Janeen Bryant

In October 2010, Barack Obama is in his second year of his presidency and the issue of immigration has not only become a heated and controversial topic but also an emotional one for many people. Approximately 10.8 million undocumented people live, work, and call the United States home according to the Office of Immigration Statistics. In the minds of some, these millions not only represent a burden on the infrastructure but also a threat to the American way of life. Their presence increases the tensions in the social fabric of municipalities all across the country. Charlotte is one of them. Headlines report on the growing immigrant population and online comment sections teem with terms like "illegal" and "anchor babies." Given this climate, the Levine Museum of the New South decided to host one of several nationwide screenings of *Welcome to Shelbyville* sponsored by Welcoming America, an organization brought to our attention by the International Coalition of Sites of Conscience. As a member of the coalition's Immigration and Civil Rights Network, Levine Museum was committed to engaging museum-goers in dialogue about tough topics concerning immigration.

A few weeks after the museum signed on to host the screening, the movie arrived with a facilitator's guide, talking points, and key questions to ask before and after the screening. Along with placing chairs and setting up microphones, minutes before the guests arrived, museum staff posted inflammatory statements in the four corners of the room:

1. Immigrants take jobs away from Americans.

2. I believe there should be no limits on who can immigrate to this country.

3. Undocumented immigrants should go back where they came from.

4. Immigrants are the only reason for America's survival.

Each guest was asked to answer with a hard *yes* or *no* using a red or green dot respectively. Everyone was expected to vote before sitting down to watch the movie together. Dot by dot, the opinions of more than eighty participants were placed around the room. The museum and a range of community partners involved in immigration issues had invited participants to the screening and the conversation to follow. What resulted was a room full of people who did not know each other, who probably would never have otherwise been in the same place, much less the same row, but who now were poised to share a common experience and talk to one another.

Picture this: a Bosnian grandmother sitting next to a West African businesswoman; a native Charlottean in the seat next to an undocumented student from Mexico. Chair by chair, row after row, participants sat beneath the skylights in our two-story atrium. With a black-trimmed white screen in front of them, for forty-five minutes they watched the film, which depicts the small town of Shelbyville, Tennessee, grappling with demographic change brought about by the arrival of Somalis and Latinos and the community responses in school, church, public, work, and civic spaces. Encounters between longtime residents and newcomers revealed tension and humanity. As the credits rolled, the room was filled with a contemplative mood. The movie created a shared experience for the entire room and set a tone of reflection and reaction. Then a skilled facilitator invited visitors to respond to the themes of the film and to engage in dialogue with each other.

As the movie came to a close, vice president of education, Janeen Bryant, began, "Being that almost everyone in the United States is a product of immigration, can you think of any similarities in the film with your own family's immigration story?" The first question inspired the grandmother to talk about the many ways the movie resonated with her experience of isolation and disconnection from her homeland. Many in the audience affirmed her statement with head nods, whispers, and a few claps. The sharing commenced from that moment forward. For a few minutes, audience members shared how they related to the film and shared their own immigration stories. The turning point in the conversation occurred when a fifteen-year-old student from Mexico shakily stood up and asked a single question: "*Why?*" He took a deep breath, then began again: "Why do they want to treat us like this? Why do they hate my mother?" It was obvious that he had made a deeply personal connection to what was seen in the documentary and was poignantly asking not only all of the participants in the room but also the museum and the larger community. Why were immigrants being treated as criminals? Why were families being separated? Why was immigration being seen through such a vitriolic, antagonistic lens all over the country? Before his turn at the mic ended and the night was finished, he had shared with this audience of strangers united by similar experiences that one of his parents—his mother—had been deported. He remained in Charlotte unsure of his future and unsure of how to get back in contact with her.

It is moments like these when programs transcend mere educational content. Instead, they offer true opportunities to engage the community, invite participants to connect in new and unexpected ways, and explore together how a moment in history can shape the future civic fabric. Seeing the impact of immigration on our neighbors and our communities has been the catalyst for much of the dialogic work Levine Museum has undertaken in recent years. Immigration is challenging for communities in nearly every corner of the United States. This is likely to continue even if reform manages to stem undocumented immigration because over half of the newcomers are here legally and scholars say that global population flows will inevitably grow—a consequence of the world's increasingly globalized economy and political unrest and war around the world.

This change has become more and more evident in the South. Once the nation's most isolated region, largely bypassed by the great waves of European immigration from the 1880s to the 1910s, today the southeastern United States is America's fastest growing immigrant destination. Sunbelt economic growth in the past few decades has made the region a magnet for newcomers from across the United States and around the globe. During the 1990s, the Brookings Institution reported that the nation's four "Hispanic hyper-growth cities" were all in the Southeast: Raleigh, Greensboro, and Charlotte in North Carolina, plus Atlanta, Georgia. By the 2000s, southeastern localities held eight of the ten top spots for such growth. [1]

Charlotte, which had little experience with immigration during most of the twentieth century, found itself one of the fastest growing new immigrant destinations in the nation. Its foreign-born population grew from under 4 percent in 1990 to 15 percent in 2015. Nielsen cited Charlotte as the fastest growing Latino metro market in the nation between 2000 and 2010.[2] Although Latinos are the largest and most visible segment, representing just over half of Charlotte's immigrants, roughly a quarter of the city's immigrants are Asian, 10 percent are from Africa, and another 10 percent are from Europe. Like other new immigrant gateway cities, Charlotte's immigrant settlement is happening within a suburban context. Charlotte has no tight-packed tenements like "Little Italy" or "Chinatown." Instead, the newcomers are intermingled with each other and with native-born whites and blacks in sprawling post–World War II suburbs.[3] Immigration scholar Roberto Suro, formerly of the Pew Hispanic Center and now with the University of Southern California, predicts that future historians may well look to Charlotte as *the* bellwether for how America addresses issues of immigrant growth in the early twenty-first century.

From 2005 to 2007, Levine Museum of the New South staff members were becoming increasingly aware of immigration as more and more diverse newcomers arrived and new cultural currents influenced our community. Students from more than one hundred countries, speaking more than 150 languages other than English, now attended our public schools and visited the museum on field trips. Almost daily, we observed examples of how new cultures were enriching and enlivening our city and also sparking friction and tension as people with different traditions, habits, and assumptions encountered one another. We began asking ourselves: How will our community respond to diverse newcomers and the new ethnic geography of our region? For a city and a region long known for its black and white racial landscape, what does the new multicultural, multiethnic reality mean for our collective future? What role can a museum play in deepening cross-cultural understanding and fostering a more accessible and inclusive community?

To address these crucial issues, Levine Museum in mid-2007 launched the Newcomer Project, a multiyear effort to create an interactive exhibit, complementary programming, and civic dialogue. The museum's goals were to increase awareness and understanding of the dramatic demographic and cultural changes our city was experiencing and to give people across the Charlotte region multiple ways to come together to share their stories, find new connections, and forge social capital. Bringing people of different backgrounds together for interaction and dialogue was integral to all aspects of the project. All components of the initiative were designed to spark community conversation across cultural boundaries.

Generous grants from the Charlotte-Mecklenburg Community Foundation and the John S. and James L. Knight Foundation allowed for two years of research and planning with community partners, talking and listening. Noted exhibition developer Darcie Fohrman, who had joined the museum on our award-winning *Courage* exhibition on school desegregation, came back to guide the process. Our approach was to make the exhibition for everyone. It had to be something that bridged "us" and "them." We settled on a theme that everyone—natives and newcomers, US- and foreign-born alike—was grappling with: cultural change. Additionally, in 2008, Levine Museum was invited to become an inaugural member of the Immigration and Civil Rights Network of the International Coalition of Sites of Conscience. The coalition convened participating museums from across the country to share their dialogic models and their relationships to the unique community contexts and the histories of their regions. Representatives of museums, historic houses, sites of memory, and national parks sites shared their processes and models using each other as critics and observers. What emerged was a rich cross-pollination of traditional programming and innovative dialogic approaches tested by veteran museum personnel and their novice counterparts.

Through this exposure to a variety of dialogue models, it became clear that the process of examining immigration as a civil right opened a unique dialogic space for Southern museums, particularly those institutions willing to counter larger historic narratives with the stories of individuals encountering immigration as both an insurmountable system and as a reality of their daily lives. The experiences were not ethnic, race, age, or gender specific. Instead, they offered a chance to ask the questions key to development of any person moving to a new place.

In February 2009, the Newcomer Project culminated with the opening of a new 3,500-square-foot exhibition *Changing Places: From Black and White to Technicolor* and the launch of twenty months of robust public programming. Exhibition design encouraged discussion around key questions heard in local media, civic forums, and through word of mouth. Each learning environment of the exhibition was organized around a critical question or theme encouraging guests to reflect on their possible answers and to consider the answers of others as they make the South their home. Writing in the journal *Curator*, Dr. Jeff Hayward, director of People, Places & Design Research, Northampton, Massachusetts, gave this assessment of the exhibition's dialogic impact:

> The exhibit is not a presentation of cultures; it's a dialog with its community. . . . I was struck by the plethora of "talk back" boards with local voices, personal connections and experiences, emotional and intellectual outpourings. . . . The dialog also comes from the Story Kiosk, a video booth where children and adults record their comments about the

exhibition; that was well-used, popular, and engaging (clips are played back on a nearby flat screen video, and posted on YouTube). Examples of barriers in cultural interaction were presented so clearly that I came away with a sense of how astonishingly simple it would be to change some of the practices we (mainstream American culture) perpetuate because of our ignorance. I knew about and had personal experience with customs such as offering tea to a visitor, handshaking and bowing as greetings, and how close to stand for a conversation, but yet this exhibition gave me such straightforward explanations that when I went home I enjoyed telling them to my friends.

Dr. Hayward went on to say that:

This project sets a high standard to emulate for other cultural diversity projects. It doesn't just "tell a story" about cultural change, it provides a platform for local residents, and for out-of-town visitors like myself, to put personal experience ahead of cultural stereotypes, and to expand our ability to communicate and empathize with people we don't know, without necessarily being aware that we are respecting our differences.[4]

In conjunction with the opening of the *Changing Places* exhibition, Levine Museum launched a major dialogue initiative designing models for both adults and youth: *Speaking of Change* and *Turn the Tables* respectively. Starting as a pilot, the latter was the museum's first dialogue-based programming for teens. *Turning the Tables* attracted fifty-two groups and 1,221 participants. *Speaking of Change* was a dialogue model for adults designed by Octavia Seawell of OZS Consulting in partnership with Charlotte's Community Building Initiative, Levine Museum staff, and faculty from the University of North Carolina at Charlotte. The model had four objectives: (1) allow participants to reflect on personal reactions to *Changing Places* and its themes about life in a dynamic, multicultural city; (2) articulate those reactions to others; (3) connect more authentically as a group; and (4) consider what they may want to do as a result. Seawell worked collaboratively with the museum to design the adult dialogic experience and facilitator trainings.

The design of the *Speaking of Change* model built upon successes and learning gleaned from previous dialogue-based programming at Levine Museum. In many ways, it refined the approach originally tested in 2004 with *Conversations on Courage*. Key features included:

- a 2.5-hour experience, including an exhibit visit in silence followed by facilitated dialogue

- use of multiple points of access including individual reflection, paired conversation, and facilitated discussion with the whole group

- limitation of group size to twelve to twenty-five participants

- extensive facilitator training and support

- recruitment of intact affinity groups from many sectors

The opportunity to gain "a deeper understanding of Charlotte as a dynamic multicultural city and be inspired to explore that diversity"[5] proved to be an attractive offering. More than 1,600 individuals in 118 groups participated in *Speaking of Change* dialogues, coming from businesses, churches, nonprofits, schools, local government, and community organizations. Almost all sessions were made up of people who worked together, served on a board together, attended the same congregation, or belonged to a common organization. There were two notable exceptions. The first exception included a session for elected officials attended by the mayor, the chair of the county commission, and the chair of the school board along with other local elected leaders. The second exception included the publishers of the *Charlotte Observer*, the *Charlotte Post*, *Las Noticias*, and the *Asian Herald* along with senior staff members of their respective papers. Interestingly, Mecklenburg County decided to make *Speaking of Change* an integral component of its diversity training for its employees. More than four hundred county staff members in fourteen groups participated, representing all of the county's departments.

University of North Carolina at Charlotte faculty members Dr. Heather Smith and Dr. Susan Harden with the help of research assistant Paul McDaniel executed the evaluation strategy for more than a year. Researchers observed twelve dialogues documenting both process and content and collected and analyzed more than a thousand self-reported, post-dialogue paper surveys. The findings in UNC Charlotte's evaluation of *Speaking of Change* point to a positive impact:[6]

- 76.2 percent of participants indicated that they felt the *Changing Places* exhibition was mostly or extremely valuable.

- 74.8 percent of participants indicated they felt the *Speaking of Change* dialogues and reflection time after viewing the exhibition was mostly or extremely valuable.

Evaluation revealed that participants were overwhelmingly either white or black, highly educated, middle class or affluent, employed, and predominantly English speakers. Given the kinds of leadership groups recruited for the dialogues, this result is not surprising, but it is clear that the influence of the adult dialogues was concentrated on the receiving community and not among immigrants.

Evaluation highlights included participants self-reporting that the "Getting Past Us and Them" learning environment was the most impactful. In this dimly lit section of the exhibition, dialogue participants were asked to enter the space in silence and watch videos of diverse teens describing how they had been stereotyped and bullied at school. Silhouettes of an undocumented family stood silently as a newsreel played a continuous loop of headlines related to immigration, documentation status, assimilation, wage theft, and other topics associated with increased immigration to the South and the tensions that have come with this increase. Key findings from the 2010 evaluation report of *Speaking of Change* include:

- There was awareness that migrants—whether national or international—have hybrid cultures that reflect elements from all the places in which they have settled or been raised.

- People who have moved around a lot often end up with a blended set of cultural affiliations in the way they self-identify, act, and speak and in their perspectives.

- Immigrants often maintain ties to their home cultures, but take things from their new cultures in their destination area and add this to their own personal cultural identity.

- One immigrant participant expressed cultural identity in a slightly different way—emphasizing the point that culture is fluid and sometimes intersectional.[7]

Two follow-up dialogue sessions, one of county employees and one of non-county participants, indicated that participants were influenced by *Speaking of Change* dialogues to enact inclusive behaviors and actions at the individual, organizational, and community levels, though the overwhelming majority (78 percent) of actions cited were individual actions. Here are some of the individual actions participants listed:

- I was able to use concepts from the Us/Them portion of the exhibit with a youth group for Sunday school.

- I use language in more thoughtful ways.

- I talk more about who I am.

- I came to an MLK celebration at the museum with my daughter.

- I'm doing more reaching out as a black person to white groups.

- I recommend the exhibit.

The following are organizational and community examples participants gave:

- At work, we talk about differences more.

- We created a diversity committee in our workplace.

- I facilitated a march for Justice and Peace.

- I created a dialogue between African American churches and immigrants on immigrant issues.

Evaluation was key in helping Levine Museum staff understand the effectiveness of the *Speaking of Change* model and the power of dialogue to act as a catalyst in our community.

Having a "third thing" to react to opens people up to talk about uncomfortable topics. Whether a film, exhibition, or something else, an emotionally powerful experience evokes personal stories and reactions and promotes receptive listening. Such shared storytelling fosters feelings of safety and connection that often didn't exist beforehand. It moves people in unexpected ways and allows them to explore difficult issues that previously seemed too contentious to address head-on. We also learned that engaging immigrant communities takes sustained effort and cultural sensitivity. While *Changing Places* set attendance records and attracted a notably more ethnically diverse audience, we were disappointed that Latinos did not visit in significant numbers during the first twelve months, despite partnering with numerous Latino community organizations, featuring in the exhibition Latino stories, music, and a re-created *tienda*, and having exhibition labels written in Spanish, Spanish subtitles in all videos, and a gallery guide written in Spanish. We learned that building relationships is vital and subsequently embarked on a multiyear initiative, the Latino New South project, to listen and learn with diverse Latinos about how museums can be resources for them, their families, and their organizations.

In new immigrant gateways like Charlotte, North Carolina, with little or no experience of immigrant integration, cultural institutions can play a major role in:

- building awareness of growing multiculturalism and the reasons that lie behind it

- helping community members develop new skills, knowledge, and ways of thinking

- providing opportunities for cross-cultural interactions that build relationships and shared meaning

In presenting to the national Urban Affairs Association in 2011 about *Speaking of Change*, UNC Charlotte scholars argued that "cultural and educational institutions play a critical, but often overlooked role in guiding community response to newcomer arrival." In an essay in the journal *Museums and Social Issues*, the *Changing Places* exhibition and *Speaking of Change* dialogues were cited as examples of "museum programming that is deepening understanding of immigration in ways that led to a warmer welcome and proactive inclusion . . . guiding community receptivity towards immigrants in a way that provides counterbalance to reactive and hostile responses." Additionally, with the "appointment of an Immigrant Integration Task Force, Charlotte publicly appears to be heading in a direction of warmer receptivity and the museum continues to shape the process." The Levine Museum president at the time, Emily Zimmern, was appointed as vice chair of the task force, and in the analysis of the researchers, "her selection is a direct result of Levine Museum's community collaborations for *Changing Places* and the Latino New South project."

BOX 2.1.

SPEAKING OF CHANGE PROCESS

- Group overview outside the exhibit
- Exhibit viewing
- One-word reaction from group members just outside exhibit exit
- Break and move to dialogue room
- Silent reflection on five questions
- Overview/guidelines/introductions (see below)
- Talk in pairs about responses to questions
- Full group dialogue
- Closure/feedback

Dialogue Guidelines

- Focus on understanding your own thoughts and reactions to the exhibit.
- Listen to understand the thoughts and feelings of others without judgment, though they may be different from your own.
- Ask questions to seek understanding of others. Summarize what you think you're hearing.
- Be curious and open to change as you hear others.
- Avoid overanalyzing and problem solving.
- Share "air-time."
- Honor confidentiality.

©Courtesy of OZS Consulting
Used with permission.

We also learned that change is often unsettling. *Speaking of Change* deepened the conversation and made it less unsettling. The entire *Newcomers Project* showed that as seismic demographic shifts are transforming our country and our community, museums have the opportunity to play a vital civic role. Modeling inclusion and collaboration, they can provide safe spaces for dialogue and cross-cultural experiences. They can create transcendent moments like the one in 2010 when a young student shared his family's story. With a focus on our changing communities, we can build cross-cultural connections, we can rethink the idea that where we come from shapes who we are, and we can celebrate the diversity in our midst.

BOX 2.2.

QUESTIONS FOR SILENT REFLECTION

1. What word or phrase describes how you "feel" leaving the exhibit?
2. Do you feel that you have a clear cultural identity? If so, what is it?
3. a. What aspect of the exhibit made you feel some discomfort (anxiety, confusion, overwhelm, concern, resistance, disagreement)?
   b. What in your personal values or experience might cause that response?
3. What's the most significant learning for you personally from the exhibit?
4. a. What aspect of yourself has changed or might change as a result of being in a multicultural environment?
   b. What about your identity/heritage/beliefs do you most want to hold on to?
   c. Why is it important to hold on to?

BOX 2.3.

AFTER SILENT REFLECTION

Overview/Introductions: Ten to fifteen minutes

Stop participants even if they have not completed all the questions. Welcome them again and refer them to the back of the cover page. Review the dialogue process (back of cover page) indicating where they are in the process. Review the guidelines. Emphasize confidentiality. Ask for a nod or thumbs up as a sign of agreement.

Ask participants to say their name, role in the organization (if appropriate), and how long they have lived in Charlotte. Include yourself.

Conversation in Pairs: Thirteen minutes

Ask participants to pair up with someone they don't know well or who may have a different background. Encourage them to get up out of their chair and move to that person, not just turn to the person sitting next to them. If there's an uneven number, there will be a trio (and thus less time for each person to talk). Tell them they can move through all questions with one person and then switch to the other person or go back and forth with the questions.

Hearing from Pairs: Twelve minutes

Give pairs a one-minute warning and ask them to be prepared to give a headline report out of something (a theme) that stood out from their conversation. Call time and begin to hear from pairs. Keep report out to a minute. If there's time, ask if the other person has something to add. Briefly summarize what you heard. Ask a follow-up question if appropriate. LISTEN . . . make notes if you'd like. What themes emerge? Are there similarities or differences?

Dialogue: Thirty to forty minutes

Get them back into a tight circle.

You can ask them about something they heard from pairs that they would like to talk more about or you can identify something that emerged from one or more pairs, comment on it, and ask a question.

Keep the focus personal. Avoid going into a critique of the exhibit. If a participant brings up things about the exhibit (positive or negative), ask how/why that impacted them personally. Listen for stories and allow personal stories to emerge . . . either about background/history or how they're experiencing multicultural Charlotte today . . . its impact on them. Explore differences in stories. Help them make meaning.

Ensure that most if not everyone talks. Don't allow one person or perspective to dominate. Ask: "What do others think about that?" Or "Do others have a different perspective or viewpoint?" Find a place to summarize and perhaps leave a few questions with the group.

BOX 2.4.

THEMES THAT MAY EMERGE

Identity:

What does the term mean? Do I have a cultural identity? Is my cultural identity only where I've come from or my race/ethnicity, or is it larger? Difference in how I see myself and how others see me?

Stories:

This, along with identity, is the key focus of the dialogue. Hearing each other's stories. Deepening our understanding of each other.

Change:

How much? How fast? Impact of change? How do I deal with change? Am I personally aware of it, touched by it? Living in a bubble?

Who's in the exhibit?

Do white people (particularly Southern white women) have a cultural identity or interesting story? What is it? What about African Americans descended from enslaved people? Native Americans? How do they fit in the past and the present?

Religion:

Is it an inclusive or exclusive aspect of local culture?

Stereotype:

What's the truth in them? Am I stereotyped? How do we deal with them? Can we get past them?

Immigrants:

What's it like to come here from a home you know and love? How are those who have been here responding? Are Northerners who move to Charlotte considered immigrants? In what way?

Holding on and letting go:

What does each of us hold on to? What has each of us let go of? What do we want or need to let go of?

Language:

Both as a barrier and as a way to connect.

BOX 2.5.

QUESTIONS THAT CAN HELP MOVE THE DIALOGUE ALONG

Last two questions on the questions for reflection.

How many of you could easily identify your cultural identity? How many could not? What does this say about us?

Did you see your story reflected in the exhibit in some way? If so, in what way? If not, how did you feel?

Where do you personally most feel the impact of change to a more diverse, multicultural community?

Is your group reflective of multicultural Charlotte? In what way? Why or why not?

Closure and "Check Out": Five to seven minutes

Bring the dialogue to a close. Ask a question that you want each person to answer briefly (thirty minutes each). Something like: "What's a key takeaway from the exhibit and dialogue process today?," "Is there anything you'd like to do differently as a result of your experience today?," or "Any choices that you might make differently now?" Or something else that emerges . . .

Emphasize that we are not looking for big changes: it could be something as simple as reading something, bringing family to the exhibit and having a conversation with them, exploring another part of town, having a deeper conversation with someone, exploring personal history, or simply reflecting more. Give them an example or two that feel appropriate for the group.

Survey/Feedback Form: Five minutes

Explain that the form has been developed and that data collected will be summarized by UNC–Charlotte.

Notes

1. Roberto Suro and Audrey Singer, "Changing Patterns of Latino Growth in Metropolitan America," in *Redefining Urban and Suburban America: Evidence from Census 2000*, ed. Bruce Katz and Robert Lang (Washington, DC: Brookings Institution Press, 2004), 190–94.

2. "Latino Populations Are Growing Fastest Where We Aren't Looking," Nielsen Newswire, May 1, 2013, http://www.nielsen.com/us/en/insights/news/2013/latino-populations-are-growing-fastest-where-we-arent-looking.html.

3. Suro and Singer, "Changing Patterns of Latino Growth in Metropolitan America," 190–94.

4. Jeff Hayward, "Connecting a Museum with Its Community," *Curator Journal* 53 (2010), doi: 10.1111/j.2151-6952.2010.00048.x.

5. *Speaking of Change* Brochure.

6. S. Harden, H. Smith, and P. McDaniel, "*Speaking of Change* Evaluation Report for the Levine Museum of the New South" (Charlotte, 2010).

7. Ibid., 65.

TALKING ABOUT IMMIGRATION WITH CHILDREN THROUGH A SOCIAL JUSTICE LENS

Linda Blanshay

Introduction

In 2008, the International Coalition of Sites of Conscience (the coalition) invited the Museum of Tolerance, Los Angeles, to join the Regional Dialogues on Immigration Network (RDI) as a participant in a national conversation on the unique role that museums can play in fostering dialogue on the pressing issue of immigration. As shown in a Pew Hispanic survey, approximately 64 percent of US Latino residents reported that the immigration debate had negatively impacted their lives, while 78 percent reported feeling that discrimination remained a problem affecting their communities.[1] It was increasingly evident in Southern California that young people were exposed to regular media representations that depicted immigration as a "problem" or, worse yet, a crime. As a museum dedicated to promoting respect and understanding, the Museum of Tolerance (MOT) eagerly joined the network to provide a new program for schools promoting meaningful and ethical discussions about immigration.

A core theme of the MOT's *Finding Our Families, Finding Ourselves* exhibit is immigration/migration with a broader focus on history, memory, and stories. It was decided that a special program would be created based on the exhibit for elementary school children, aligning to fourth- and fifth-grade content standards on late nineteenth- and early twentieth-century California and its immigration histories. Characteristic of the MOT, the program had to be more than a history lesson; it set out to enable students to apply their critical thinking skills, promote empathy, and introduce them to a broader way of thinking about immigration, then and now. Immigration would be explored through a social justice lens. During the program's pilot phase, the interpretive plan and dialogue arc were evaluated and fine-tuned with groups from three schools. The main challenge that became apparent was the need to better prepare the program's facilitators. This is always a priority in the museum, but this program prompted additional and specific self-awareness and skills training for having sensitive conversations about immigration with children.

Conscience Content

Discussions on immigration are never neutral. The historical authority of the museum made it important to carefully select the primary messages of this program through a social justice lens without employing partisan political agendas. Two important research-based themes[2] chosen for the interpretation plan were: (1) human rights: the moral imperative of treating the subject of immigration and everyone involved with compassion and respect; and (2) prosperity: the economic necessity of immigration and the contributions of immigrants.

During the many intense conferences and symposia organized by the coalition for regional network participants, additional key research-based ideas emerged from the presentations and workshops that also helped determine the learning outcomes and arc of dialogue for the MOT program:

- *Explicit connections between past and present* help students better understand the issues.

- *Freedom of movement* is a human right and challenges engrained thinking.

- *Migration is a broader concept* and a useful frame for contextualizing immigration.

- *Youth immigrant voices* are powerful in eliciting compassion and deeper listening.

- *Putting a human face on immigration* through stories is essential to creating empathy.

- *We are a nation of immigrants* narrative is not adequate for dispelling stereotypes.

Special sessions at coalition conferences featured academics and representatives from organizations such as Welcoming America. They promoted positive language such as using "neighbors" instead of always saying "immigrants" and eliminating language such as the dehumanizing term "illegal aliens."[3]

In addition to positive messaging, the program had to address embedded myths and assumptions about immigration. Research shows that by the age of three, children hold stereotypes about groups of people.[4] In Teaching Tolerance's exploration of the issue, they identified ten myths about immigration common among young people.[5] The program explicitly incorporated content that aimed to present counter-narratives and overturn four of these specific myths that students, especially in Los Angeles, may have already internalized or might come across:

- "Immigrants are less than or not 'real' Americans."

- "Immigrants take jobs from Americans."

- "The majority of immigrants in the United States are Mexican."

- "Latinos are mostly undocumented."

The challenge was to design a program that created "safety" around talking about this subject while enabling *all* students to rethink their assumptions. The goal was to normalize and contextualize immigration in a larger historical and social framework, challenging "us and them" thought patterns.

Program Outline

The museum's interactive exhibit *Finding Our Families, Finding Ourselves*, opened in 2003, celebrates diverse American family stories. It features beautiful dioramas, artifacts, and presentations by American celebrities; including poet, bestselling author, historian, and educator, Dr. Maya Angelou; award-winning actor, comedian, and director Billy Crystal;

PROGRAM HIGHLIGHTS	
PART I: INTRODUCTION AND PREDICTION	Where: classroom (thirty minutes)
	Welcome: The program opens with a welcome and introduction to the dialogue format. Students are shown a vivid image of a scene from the exhibit for a prediction activity and asked questions such as: *What's going on in this picture? What do you think this experience will be about?* People You Know Game: Students receive a handout that includes a map of the world. They are divided into small groups and asked to come up with four people (could be a famous person, family member, neighbor, teacher, etc.) who came to the United States from another country. They can use the map for hints. The game is fast-paced with only three minutes to come up with as many people as they can. The groups report their results, which are added up into a class total to show how many people they know from many parts of the world. Celebrity Guessing Game: Students receive handheld voting devices. They are shown photos of famous people (who they recognize from entertainment, sports, etc.) and have to vote whether the celebrity is an immigrant or US-born. The selection is very diverse, featuring mostly celebrities who are immigrants to the United States to make the point that immigration is common across all races/ethnicities and socioeconomic backgrounds. They learn that some of their favorite celebrities are immigrants.
PART II: JOURNEY OF DISCOVERY IN *FINDING OUR FAMILIES, FINDING OURSELVES*	Where: exhibit (sixty minutes)

PROGRAM HIGHLIGHTS	
Area: Turn of the Twentieth-Century Immigration Wave Port Scene and Beyond  	Students move from the classroom area into the exhibit experience with the transition: *There is not one immigration story. There are many and they are all American stories.* Silent Walk Activity: Students are asked to walk around the scene quietly to consider where they are and what clues they find. Pair Share: Students are broken into pairs or small groups and are assigned different map and artifact areas for discussions on topics such as facts we can learn (from maps, data, history) to likely emotions and connections to today. Journey: Students then move through a boat scene, an inspection station, and an area focused on early twentieth-century internal migration with people seeking jobs. A large group discussion is held to discuss the contributions immigrants have made throughout history, the hardships they faced, and the impact these events had on Native Americans. The next part of the exhibit features the family stories of several famous Americans as told through their own words.
Area: Maya Angelou's Room 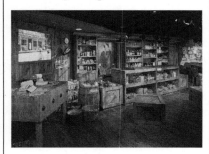	Maya Angelou's room is a re-creation of the general store where she grew up with her brother, grandmother, and great uncle. She describes why it was special to her and the values and legacy of pride she gained from her closest relatives. She also relates her family's forced migration as enslaved people to the United States, critically inserting a reminder that the immigration process and narrative is only one experience of the United States and its peoples.

PROGRAM HIGHLIGHTS	
Area: Joe Torre's Room 	Joe Torre's story focuses on his mother who emigrated from Italy as a young girl. Joined by his siblings on screen, Joe recounts the ways that his mother was his role model and taught him everything he knows about true leadership. He also recounts how she was made to feel ashamed of her immigrant background even by her own husband.
Area: Billy Crystal's Room 	Billy's story is set in a re-created painting of the tenement flat in which his father lived. With his uncle Bern helping fill him in in on his family's history, Billy Crystal tells the story of his father's side of the family, how they lived in New York, and how this shaped his views about the importance of family.
Area: Carlos Santana's Room 	Playing music and describing the presented documentary footage of his family, Carlos Santana describes his family's mixed heritage of Mexican descent. He tells the story of his family's immigration from Mexico to the United States, his parents' love story, and the legacy he hopes to pass on to the next generation.
PART III: SYNTHESIS AND DEBRIEF	Where: classroom (thirty minutes)
	In the final section of the program, students are given the opportunity to reflect on what they experienced and discuss it in small groups. They recall that throughout the program they heard many different types of stories of immigration and migration—from many countries, for many reasons, and with different outcomes. Two formats have been used to stimulate reflection and dialogue. One format includes arts-based activities and the other includes artifacts hidden in the pockets of a giant quilt around which the children sit. The goal of the final discussion is for students to share their expanded perspectives and reflect on how immigration is an ever-present and important part of the American experience. Ultimately, they are asked to consider how they can help all immigrants, "new neighbors," feel more welcome.

multiple Grammy winner and Rock and Roll Hall of Fame recipient Carlos Santana; and National League Most Valuable Player and former manager of the four-time World Series Champions, the New York Yankees Joe Torre. The illuminating stories they share reflect the lives and dreams of the family members who came before them and inspired them to greatness today. The installation encourages visitors to seek out their own histories, mentors, and heroes.

Pilot Observations

The program was piloted to eight groups of fourth and fifth graders from three schools. The content passed through approvals and the evaluations from teachers were very positive. Students gave feedback through pre- and post-surveys. It was in the program observations that the real challenges and opportunities were seen. Each pilot program was observed by two staff people who watched for level of engagement, types of questions, body language, and other factors. The notes show differences in student engagement based on their own immigration histories and statuses. Not surprisingly, the same program content was experienced very differently by the diverse spectrum of student groups.

The first pilot group was completed with students from a culturally diverse but largely white area in Los Angeles. From the first map activity, the students were completely open about their family's immigration histories, mostly from European countries. While they were never asked to reveal their family's immigration histories, they immediately personalized the prompt question and offered this information readily and proudly. They were an academically high-achieving group of students who knew California history more than others of the same age. When asked, "What contributions do immigrants make?" one boy answered, "More people are paying taxes!" Many students in the group shared savvy answers and they seemed intellectually engaged in the topic and its various historical dimensions. These students were also joyful in the experience, viewing it as a fun alternative to being in the classroom.

The second pilot program was offered to a group of students from a mainly Latino neighborhood in Los Angeles. Some of these students had undocumented family members. Their body language was more reserved on arrival. They became animated at the start of the program during the map activity icebreaker, but they were less forthcoming about personal immigration stories and focused mainly on naming countries from which they knew other people came. Relative to other groups, they came up with an impressively long list of countries, showing a keen awareness of other people's origins. In the beginning of the exhibit, when asked, "What might immigrants feel or worry about before they come here?" it was observed that student answers were less factually based and more emotionally; they were explaining these issues to the program staff. There were also more answers that identified discrimination in this country as a problem that immigrants face when they arrive in the United States. This group was wide-eyed and interested but noticeably more pensive than the earlier group.

The third pilot group came from a neighborhood in Los Angeles that is home to very recent immigrants from Asian Pacific countries. Some of the students came to California in the past two years and most spoke English as a second language. They took up the challenge of the icebreaker map activity with enthusiasm but came up with less variety of countries than other groups. One might assume that they either did not yet know many people from different countries or that they had not yet realized that many people they encountered were also immigrants.

It was in this group that the facilitator was challenged to rethink what she thought was an easy question. In the Billy Crystal room of the exhibition, she asked, "Do you listen to stories about your family's history?" She was met with blank stares and the answer, "I don't hear my family's stories." She followed up with the question, "Do you think you will go home and want to hear them?" One of the students raised her hand and explained to the guide that, for most of them, their extended families were not with them in the United States and so they did not have the opportunity to do that. Some students looked sad to feel left out of what the exhibit boldly promoted: talk to your family members.

During the celebrity guessing game every group revealed unspoken assumptions about immigration. All groups made some mistakes in guessing who was an immigrant and who was not. When asked why they made those decisions, someone in each group said that "you can tell who is an immigrant." The guide reminded them that they got some answers wrong. In the group of students who were themselves mostly immigrants, one student answered, "You can tell by the size of their eyes and how white they are. White people are born from America." This was part of some of the most animated group discussions in the program. Despite the fact that they were shown photos of diverse people of all countries, socioeconomic backgrounds, and racial backgrounds, the stereotypical assumptions were engrained.

Per the research, it was expected that students had internalized stereotypes about immigrants. However, the surfacing of them so directly in the program and the apprehensions some students showed around certain questions meant that there was a responsibility to approach the subject with extreme care and sensitivity. The role of the facilitator was essential in this. Perhaps it was a testament to the safety created with each group that students allowed themselves to share their authentic feelings about the topic in front of each other and museum staff members. Certainly it brought up the need to find ways to support their emotional and psychological needs as much as possible.

It's About the Adults

Children struggle with bias and stereotypes because they learned it from the adults and social world around them. Research on prejudice in children[6] has shown that their impressions of "the other" mirror the social structures that, while unspoken, are clearly visible to all. For example, a teacher or parent may never verbalize support for segregation, but where they choose to live and which friends they choose to associate with speaks volumes to a child. Social justice education then involves naming and critically analyzing these structures.

In Southern California, teachers often share with MOT staff members that the topic of immigration is one they avoid. The heated political tenor potentially causes anxiety to them and their students. Teachers say that talking about the early history of immigration in California is a safe topic, whereas the contemporary connections are not. In the worst cases, some teachers communicate their own partisan values on this topic using biased language, skewed facts, and "colorblind" views. But most often, as with "race avoidance," teachers were relatively silent because they feared saying the wrong things.

In his book *Promoting Racial Literacy in Schools*, Howard Stevenson addresses the false assumption that silence equals noncommunication. Through micromessaging, values and opinions are transmitted through a variety of nonverbal cues: "reactions include eye-blinks, hesitation, stuttering, uncomfortable pauses, linguistic gaffs, frequently avoidant eye contact, excessive excuse-making, excessive probing for approval, inappropriate redirection of conversation, and the use of silence."[7] When teachers are not proactive about racial issues they find stressful to discuss, students are at risk for internalizing negative stereotypes that undermine self-identity and success.

The prevalence of negative messages in the media combined with the silence of educational leaders and other adult figures in children's lives set up the conditions for explicit and implicit biases and negative self-identity. The team at the Smithsonian Early Enrichment Center (SEEC) has been exploring the role of museums in helping young children establish a positive self-identity and an appreciation of others.[8] Their museum program is a resource and catalyst for learning that often does not occur in the classroom or is presented in a biased fashion. A special opportunity the museum provides is as a content resource for teachers. With the opportunity to establish positive self-identity and an appreciation of others comes the need for adults to examine their own beliefs and assumptions. It is an opportunity for "staff, volunteers and docents [to be] encouraged, even required, to think deeply about how their own social identity influences the visitors' experience."[9]

Nurturing the identity and self-perceptions of children requires a committed effort to analyze our own identities and perceptions. It also reinforces the need for customized dialogue-based approaches to allow for patient, individualized exploration for each child. There can be no single script to follow but only a thoughtful plan led by a skilled, empathic facilitator.

Docent Training: Preparing to Facilitate

Given the diversity of students visiting the museum and the fact that a majority of museum professionals and volunteers are white or largely of different backgrounds from the students they serve, docent/guide and facilitator training must foster self-reflection and self-awareness. It also requires us to have difficult conversations among ourselves first.

Creating a Safer Space

In the past, many sensitive and dedicated guides have asked students in the exhibit, "Who here is an immigrant?" Most of the time this question was received well, with a lot of eager hands waving in the air. Sometimes it was met with distinct shrinking body language and fear. It was decided that this personal question would no longer be asked. If students wanted to talk about their family's immigration history, there would be many opportunities to volunteer this information throughout the program without asking such a question directly. Creating safety for students means modeling respect for them and not making anyone feel singled out or exposed. Dialogue facilitation skills including compassionate listening are key to sending the unequivocal message that the museum guide is a supportive, not a judgmental, presence. Students need to be reassured through a variety of strategies that the guide will not promote an agenda that will offend them. In the MOT training program, all guides are engaged in activities to decode their own biases and positionality.

Addressing Colorblind Attitudes

In a docent training class at the MOT, one guide brought up the story of how she loved telling the students the funny story about how she (a white woman) is an immigrant and was once an "illegal alien" in the 1970s. This period occurred when she waited for her paperwork to go through after she married her American husband. She felt that sharing that story would create a connection with her group of students. This became an important training moment. The group stopped to discuss her comment and the message it sent. The facilitator asked how her story was different from the stories of undocumented students in her group. Aside from the fact that white people from Canada and European countries had privileged access to immigrate to the United States for many years, a crucial difference was that this woman was never worried about the outcome of her immigration status, whereas the students in her groups worry that they may never receive the paperwork they need to become permanent residents or citizens.

As guides and facilitators, sharing our own stories can help or hinder the process. In this case, it shut down connection and potentially offended participants. It was decided that only stories that created empathy for all could be shared. Beyond the content itself, guides have to be self-reflective in regard to their roles and how they impact the conversation itself. The first step in a docent training class must include opportunities to advance self-awareness, examine one's own lenses and biases, and uncover the implicit biases that we hold. Such a profound experience includes looking at the issues of white privilege and entitlement, colorblind attitudes, and racial anxiety.

Recognizing Microaggressions and Changing Language

In the MOT docent/facilitator training, there is a discussion that focuses on language that divides and language that uplifts. A list of positive words is introduced that should be woven throughout the experience as well as a discussion of words that should not be used. At the top of the list of words to extract from our docent vocabulary is "illegal alien." In one training session, a new volunteer (older male) decided that he was not interested in facilitating the tour because he felt it was too "politically correct." Holding this type of conversation with docents has been crucial for getting everyone on the same page regarding the values and standards of the program specifically and the museum generally. Regardless of political views, in this program, the decision was made to exclude dehumanizing language. This consideration was extended in the widest possible manner. Auditing program language is key along with a discussion of the reasons behind it. If it is the job of the docent to encourage empathy in students, they must be sure to be feeling and acting on it as well.

Conclusion

The program is a work in progress. A new component in development is the creation of activity journals, which include children's stories of immigration to California at the turn of the century and now. This will enrich the fourth- and fifth-grade academic content connections and create empathy for immigration experiences (as stories of children do), offering a chance to reflect on the experiences of immigrant children in California today. This component will also allow us to include a specific story about the migration of an indigenous family, as told by a Native American child, to add important content on the history of US displacement and migration of Native peoples. Other arts-based debriefing elements are being tested with groups for the closing synthesis and reflection portions. Ultimately, the program's positive outcomes are undoubtedly dependent on the success of the facilitator/guide in creating safety and connections with the students. A significant focus will continue to be on the ongoing professional development of guides and self-reflection that is the never-ending responsibility of museum educators for a socially just world.

Acknowledgments

With grateful thanks to the MOT team of professionals for contributions to program development and coordination: Elana Samuels, Emily Thompson, Mark Katrikh, and MOT director Liebe Geft. Special thanks to the devoted volunteers who gave advice, tested content, and tirelessly support MOT programs and the children we serve.

Notes

1. Chon A. Noriega and Francisco Javier Iiribarren, "Qualifying Hate Speech on Commercial Talk Radio: A Pilot Study," UCLA Chicano Studies Research Center Working Paper No. 1, 2011.

2. Adam Simon and Frank Gilliam, "Don't Stay on Message: What 8,000 Respondents Say about Using Strategic Framing to Move the Public Discourse on Immigration," Frameworks Institute: A Frameworks Research Report, 2013.

3. Monica Novoa, "When It Comes to Children and the Immigration Debate, Words Matter," *Colorlines: News for Action*, 2012.

4. Louise Derman-Sparks and the ABC Task Force, "Anti-Bias Curriculum: Tools for Empowering Young Children," National Association for the Education of Young Children, Washington, DC, 1989.

5. Maureen Costello, "The Human Face of Immigration" and "Ten Myths about Immigration," in *Teaching Tolerance* 39 (Spring 2011).

6. F. E. Aboud, "The Development of Prejudice in Childhood and Adolescence," in *On the Nature of Prejudice*, ed. J. F. Dovidio, P. Glick, and L. Rudman (Oxford: Blackwell, 2005), 310–26.

7. Howard C. Stevenson, *Promoting Racial Literacy in Schools* (New York: Teachers College Press, 2014), 19.

8. Betsy Bowers, Dana Brightful, Carrie Helfin, Anna Hindley, Kimberlee L. Kiehl, Erin Pruckno, Cynthia Rasno, and Jaime Wolfe, "Museums Providing Opportunities for Promoting a Positive Sense of Self in the Early Years," *Museum and Society*, 13, no. 2 (March 2015): 142–57.

9. Ibid., 147.

BETWEEN TWO WORLDS

Incubating a New Approach to Community Engagement and Civic Responsibility in an Art Museum

Suzanne Seriff[1]

Introduction

In July 2014, Gretchen Jennings, a museum professional who has blogged for several years about the need for "empathetic museums," addressed an issue on the American Alliance of Museum's website that was getting a great deal of attention in the national press at the time: tens of thousands of undocumented, unaccompanied children were crossing the US border. Her blog opened with the provocative question, "What role, if any, should museums play in this national crisis?"[2] It is a question, as Elaine Gurian and other museum critics[3] have observed, that most museums are not accustomed to asking, much less addressing. As Jennings pointed out in her blog, "There is little in our traditional structures that lends itself to timely responses to current situations." Indeed, she continued, "If we museums want to become more actively involved with our communities, especially in our fast-paced global society, we may have to develop a new process and timeline for being responsive."

Jennings proposed two ways by which she thought museums might be most effective in responding to the particular plight of unaccompanied children crossing the border and the unmet needs of undocumented immigrants in our cities more generally. First, she suggested that museums could provide *humanitarian assistance* in collaboration with experienced agencies already working in the field. She further opined that museums might be a perfect place in the public sphere to foster *discussion and dialogue* in a safe and structured environment. During the summer of 2013, when the Museum of International Folk Art's (MOIFA) Gallery of Conscience (GoC) team began to contemplate a multiyear exhibition project addressing immigrant and refugee issues, these two tactics were front and center on our minds:

- Creating a safe (or as one colleague named it, a "brave") place for dialoguing across difference

- Working collaboratively with community-based service and arts organizations to provide multiple avenues for engagement, education, assistance, and empathy

Using folk art as the starting point for both dialogue and engagement, our goal was to provide visitors and targeted community groups with the opportunity to relate to each other around the twin humanities concepts of "home" and "belonging." We planned on doing this by using the words and works of local and international folk artists who span the migration continuum: those who have left their homes to begin anew in a new land, those who have been "left behind," and those who welcome or are displaced by the new-comers in their midst.

Drawing on traditional and relatable forms of storytelling (including visual, verbal, and performing folk arts), we sought to provide a safe space for participants to address a wide range of issues affecting immigrants in this country that can be difficult to directly confront because of stigma, taboo, language barriers, stereotypes, or conflict. Not only would par-ticipants have an opportunity to engage directly with the words and works of master-level traditional artists who dare to speak out through their arts, they would also have a chance to share their own stories and personal experiences evoked by the art while being exposed to other points of view surrounding questions of home and belonging for newcomers and natives alike. Finally, we hoped to provide resources for participants to respond directly to needs they see in their own communities.

By the time the exhibition officially opened during the summer of 2014, the Gal-lery of Conscience was perfectly, if somewhat inadvertently, positioned to respond to what national headlines—and President Obama—were billing as an "urgent hu-manitarian situation."[4] Several of the artworks in the exhibition uncannily mirrored the very current events that were being spotlighted in the national news, even though they had been created years (and sometimes decades) before. Two of the most evoca-tive artworks at the time included a painting by Cuban artist Cenia Guttiérez Alfonso depicting an unaccompanied young girl crossing the Atlantic Ocean on her journey to a new land (photo 4.1) and a three-part sculpture by Peruvian American *retablo* maker Nicario Jiménez (provocatively titled *Immigration: The American Dream*), which pro-vided a critical visual commentary on what he saw as the differing receptions by Ameri-can authorities of refugees/immigrants arriving from three Hispanic countries: refugee assistance agencies for Cubans, detention centers for Haitians, and border police for Mexican families attempting to cross US borders. Putting the national "humanitarian crisis" within a global perspective was a painted wood sculpture by Mozambican folk artist Camurdino Mustafa Jetha depicting a group of "*refugiados*"—refugees from the decades-long civil war in his country—marching single file toward asylum with the barest necessities balanced on their heads (photo 4.2).

The artworks were divided into four main thematic sections based on input from community members and advisors. The four sections were titled "Deciding to Leave," "Dangerous Journeys," "Who Belongs?" and "Where Is My Home?" The theme of each section was reinforced by a first-person quote from a community member who had par-ticipated in a dialogue session about the topic. These quotes were printed in large type on computer paper and taped to the gallery walls above each section title:

Photo 4.1. *Menina con gallo/Young Girl with Rooster,* **2013. By Cenia Gutiérrez Alfonso. Cienfuegos, Cuba.**
Museum of International Folk Art, museum purchase with funds from the Barbara Lidral bequest, A.2013.46.1. Photo by Blair Clark.

- "What is the story of those who don't make it?"

- "You need to distinguish between feeling unwelcome and being unwelcome."

- "There's the home that you have made and there's the home you come from— that's always your instinctive home—where you understand it without words."

Photo 4.2. *Refugiados/Refugees*, 2013. **By Camurdino Mustafa Jetha. Santo Domasio, Mozambique.**
Museum of International Folk Art, museum purchase with funds from the Barbara Lidral Bequest, A.2013.61.2. Photo by Blair Clark.

- "When I die, throw my ashes in the Rio Grande. The ashes will decide where I belong: Mexico or the United States."

And the participatory exercises set up throughout the gallery intentionally encouraged visitors, especially young visitors, to put themselves in newcomers' shoes with prompts such as the following:

- "If you had to leave your home and could only bring what you could carry, what would it be?"

- "Describe a time when you felt that you didn't belong. Use the Post-Its or tweet your response at: @galleryofconscience." (Photo 4.3)

Even the exhibition title, *Between Two Worlds: Folk Artists Reflect on the Immigrant Experience*, was the result of a crowd-sourced contest to pick the title that best reflected the questions of "Who Belongs?" and "Who Can Be an American?" These are the very questions that have always been at the heart of the immigration debate in our nation, and they were certainly the upmost questions in our minds during the immigration "crisis" of tens of thousands of unaccompanied children who were traveling from Central and South America and crossing the US-Mexico border when the exhibition opened in 2014.

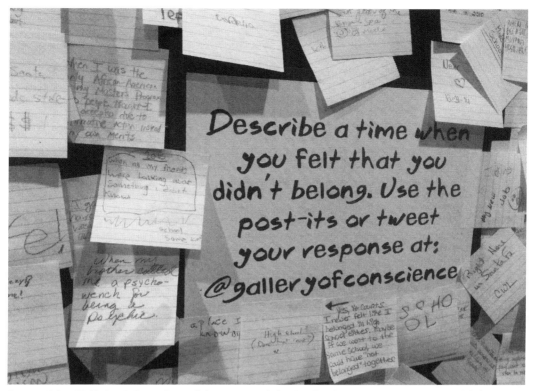

Photo 4.3. Talk back board participatory activity in the *Between Two Worlds* exhibit at the Gallery of Conscience.
Courtesy of Museum of International Folk Art Archives [Exhibitions Collection, Between Two Worlds Series AR.00004.259]. Photo by Suzanne Seriff, 2015.

The opening weeks of the *Between Two Worlds* exhibition that summer saw a flurry of activities both within and outside the gallery walls. These activities included talks and demonstrations by exhibition artists; a workshop with an international peace camp for Palestinian, Israeli, and New Mexican young women; dialogues between local and international folk artists; walk-in visits from thousands of individuals and families from both inside and outside of the state; and hands-on art and activity tours for hundreds of Native, Hispanic, immigrant, and refugee children and families from social service and arts agencies across New Mexico. Some of the organizations that participated in the opening activities and whose contributions became part of the exhibition included Literacy Volunteers of Santa Fe, Refugee Well Being Project of Albuquerque, Name Pueblo, Moving Arts Espanola, Santa Fe School for the Arts, PBJ Family Services of Albuquerque, New Mexico Asian Family Center, Big Brothers/Big Sisters of Northern New Mexico, and Northern NM Youth Works.

Although not intentionally programmed, the topic of most interest, discussion, and activity during these early weeks mirrored the topic most featured in the national news: the tens of thousands of women and children—most seeking asylum from conditions of life-threatening violence in their home countries—who had crossed the border into the United States and were being held (in many cases) in newly opened, privately run detention centers in both New Mexico and Texas. Both the design and framework of the Gallery of Conscience's *Between Two Worlds* exhibition seemed to have succeeded in providing a safe—and spontaneous—space for diverse visitors to dialogue about this controversial issue and a platform through which community agencies could effectively collaborate with the museum to offer programs and activities for affected families and individuals. Responses from visitors to the gallery were immediate and enthusiastic. Here are several samples of those visitor responses:

- "I think the topic of this exhibit is especially relevant now, with what's going on now. Makes you think about what's going on beyond the headlines. This is more personal. We can learn through individual stories. That is what is enjoyable about history—getting into the personal perspective, beyond the big picture."

- "This exhibition is very relevant to what's going on today, considering immigration law, etc. Yes, it's a very important topic. We're all immigrants in some way. It asks you to think differently about everything in the museum, not just this gallery. The show, in a very down to earth and practical way, bridges the intellectual and art appreciation with actual, real world experiences. There should be a place in every museum where you have to commit your own opinions. More museums should get a hold of people emotionally, not just intellectually."

- "This is an excellent and timely exhibit. It brings awareness and helps people empathize by putting them in others' shoes."

- "Thank you for being here. Thanks for doing this. It makes sense for MOIFA to do this exhibit because Santa Fe is a place of convergence. It offers a nice opportunity to reflect on or participate in questions like what you would take with you (if you had to leave your home suddenly). I'd like to see the exhibit as a resource for immigrants, so if someone is an immigrant, s/he can take from it and build on it. It's helpful to feel that you're not alone."

Through this exhibition project, we seemed to have captured that quality of "nimbleness" or "responsiveness" that museum professionals are beginning to recognize as necessary if their institutions are going to be able to effectively respond to timely issues as they arise, a quality one expert defines as "Agile. Sprightly. Light. Lively. Able to turn on a dime."[5] However, as these same museum professionals know, these tactics—however "sprightly" they might seem to the public—cannot be put in place overnight. Indeed, the "new process and timeline for being responsive" that Jennings alludes to is one that the Museum of International Folk Art had been slowly and conscientiously incubating for years. And, admittedly, this incubation came not without its share of bumps, hurdles, and hard knocks along the way.

Conceptualization[6]

It began in 2010 with the inauguration of the Gallery of Conscience as a dedicated space within the Museum of International Folk Art to explore timely social justice and human rights issues through the words and works of international folk artists. In some ways, this seemed to be a natural extension of the original mission of the museum, which opened its doors in 1953 on Santa Fe's famed Museum Hill. Its founder, Florence Dibell Bartlett, was witness to two world wars and a firm believer in the idea that folk art—the everyday arts of the people—was the key to promoting cultural understanding worldwide. Her words have greeted visitors to the museum for over a half a century: "The art of the craftsmen is the bond between the peoples of the world." In keeping with this tradition, MOIFA's former director Dr. Marsha Bol inaugurated the new Gallery of Conscience in the summer of 2010 as a way to make those connections even stronger. "As the largest folk art museum in the world," she noted, "we have a responsibility to use our resources to impact and strengthen our communities through the power of folk art to educate, illuminate, and connect people around powerful issues of conscience in our lives."[7]

Within its first three years, the Gallery of Conscience featured three guest-curated and professionally designed exhibitions, each of which focused on an issue of conscience explored through the words and works of traditional artists: women's empowerment (2010), natural disaster (2011), and internment in times of war (2012). The inaugural exhibition, *Empowering Women: Artisan Cooperatives that Transformed Communities,*[8] subsequently traveled to museums throughout the United States and to the Canadian Museum for Human Rights in Winnipeg. Its positive reception, both at home and on tour, attracted widespread publicity and support for the gallery, including a generous endowment from a local family that provided a financial base for future investments and innovations.

While the GoC's first three exhibitions were certainly more socially relevant and inclusive, the top-down method of curation, design, artist selection, and programmatic development was not. Both artists and community members made it clear that they wanted more. What they asked for in particular was our institutional help in creating a forum for continuing to dialogue about challenging social issues, engaging underserved and at-risk communities in more meaningful ways, and extending the conversation to explore and advocate in order to impact these issues in our own "backyard." There seemed to be something, ironically enough, about the polished and professional nature of the finished exhibitions that prevented audiences, artists, and community members from engaging as spontaneously, deeply, or personally as they would have liked. So in the fall of 2012, MOIFA took the next leap to transform the gallery into what it hoped would be an even more effective and inviting platform for genuine community engagement and collaboration. What the staff discovered was that in order to invite and welcome that kind of community consciousness, it had to do more than just alter the nature of the topics it addressed. As an institutional space, it had to really *embody* the kind of honest, engaged, collaborative, and nimble environment that it hoped to promote. This is where the idea of "incubation" really began.

Creating a Museum Incubator for Social Change

Museum consultant Kathleen McLean describes a museum incubator as "a controlled environment in which exhibition professionals can experiment with nimble processes and responsive ideas, and *practice* creating exhibitions and programs in new ways."[9] She recognizes that there are as many motivations for such a process as there are museums willing to try it out. Just a few of the many reasons that institutions have made the decision to incubate new processes include their perceived need to increase visitor engagement, attract new kinds of audiences, convey ideas in a more effective manner, or increase community investment. While motivations differ widely, so too do the means and methods for experimenting with innovative techniques. Sometimes such experiments are nothing more than a day-long workshop or a summer program in the basement of a museum. In other cases, as with the Gallery of Conscience, the museum is able to dedicate an entire gallery or wing for ongoing installations and activities that incubate new techniques of design or engagement.

Whatever form the incubation takes or whatever its underlying motivation, a museum incubator usually starts with some sort of rapid prototyping process that is tailored to the specific museum, situation, and participants. Prototyping allows for the institution to experiment with new ideas, keeping those that work, and tossing out or modifying those that don't. This is done in a way that is relatively low risk, low cost, and low maintenance. Prototypes, according to McLean, are "ideas and activities with physicality—elements with which people can interact and which can be immediately altered to improve their effect. And it is the combination of physicality, interaction, and iteration," she emphasizes, "that is most valuable in informing museum incubator ideas and designs."[10] For the Gallery of Conscience, the motivation to incubate an entirely new design process was to create a "medium" that fundamentally mirrored the "message." Like social justice work itself, we wanted a process that was responsive, responsible, collaborative, engaged, equitable, impactful, and ethically motivated.

For such a conceptual overhaul to be successful and embraced, we knew the audience and local communities needed to gain a sense of ownership through active involvement, not passive lectures. Everyone has something to offer. If we wanted to tap that collaborative vein, we had to clean our own house by shaking up the traditional museum decision-making structure. So we began by throwing out the more conventional curator/designer/educator model of exhibition expertise in favor of a team approach that was fundamentally collaborative, improvisational, and flexible. After three years of working with MOIFA as a guest curator and strategic planning consultant, I was charged with assembling such a team to lead a totally new kind of prototyping process based on visitor, artist, and community input and exchange. The six-member team ultimately consisted of three MOIFA staff members, including an educator, curator, and preparator, and two additional part-time consultants and myself as GoC director. Kathy McLean came on board as our prototyping guru consultant and veteran folklorist Laura Marcus Green was hired as our community engagement coordinator for the GoC. The revolutionary structure of our approach involved a collaborative protocol with all six team members writing labels, designing spaces, engaging visitors, creating programs, evaluating responses, and adjusting for increased clarity and depth of response after each iteration.

Like a jazz song, we began with a single social justice thread of an idea then used a few artworks to effectively explore the "melody." That first incubation year, the topic in the Gallery of Conscience was HIV/AIDS and our goal was to explore the many ways in which traditional artists and local communities use storytelling and material arts to educate, advocate, and increase awareness about HIV/AIDS both on a local and on an international scale. That year, on World AIDS Day, over a dozen works of art started the conversation. These artworks included pieces like:

- a tower of six hundred beaded dolls representing the children orphaned by AIDS in one South African village;

- an AIDS Memorial Quilt block commemorating eight New Mexicans who died at the height of the pandemic in the United States, and;

- a carved wooden sculpture of an AIDS protest march in Mozambique's capital.

Improvisation can bring out many emotions; in this case, it captured and conveyed grief, resilience, activism, and hope. People of all ages across the community responded to the call, adding miniature protest signs, memorials to loved ones, radio pieces about their own life stories, and squares later sewn into a community quilt. The year-long project provided the community with an opportunity to discuss a subject too often hidden by silence, stigma, and misinformation. The exhibition, which went through four separate iterations and changes, was neither finished nor polished; rather it was a kind of "call and response" lab in which visitors, artists, and targeted community members could come together to riff off of the initial artworks, dialogue about issues, share their thoughts, and contribute to an ongoing, iterative experience that was community-created.

We experimented with a number of techniques designed to encourage visitors to feel part of an ongoing process and able to engage easily, immediately, and meaning-fully. We taped computer-generated label text directly on the wall and used existing cases, furniture, and leftover paint colors from a previous exhibit. We displayed pho-tographs of the artwork if we didn't own the "real thing" or when we weren't sure if the real thing would be effective in engaging our audiences. And we hired a young blackboard graphic designer from Trader Joe's to literally hand-write the exhibition title and section headings in chalk directly on the gallery walls. The opening label outside the exhibition's doors invited visitors to come in, share their thoughts, try their hands, and leave their opinions, stating: "THIS IS AN EXPERIMENT. EV-ERYTHING HERE IS A WORK IN PROGRESS."

We would be doing a disservice if we didn't admit that the results of this first incubated exhibition were both exhilarating and exasperating. Challenges arose in defining exactly what we meant by "community involvement" and what we meant by "art," workflow expectations and responsibilities among team members were hard to manage, and we were challenged to effectively convey to patrons and visitors (all of whom were accustomed to experiencing highly polished and professionally designed exhibitions) the value of a work in progress. Docents wrote letters of protest, curators held closed-door meetings with the museum director, designers threatened to quit, collaborators called it a "downer," guards got nervous, funders lobbied complaints, and longtime patrons spread the word that this prototype was "the ugliest exhibit MOIFA has ever done!" Yet responses from first-time visitors, community workshop participants, and featured folk artists told a different tale. Here are some examples of what they had to say:

- "I saw myself here for the first time. Thank you for that. . . ."

- "I love that the Gallery is always changing, and is changed by the people who have responded. . . ."

- "This is a brave thing to do. . . ."

- "Look what I did!"

- "This is a beautiful exhibit—accessible in ways museums haven't felt before."

The incubated project showed that success for the gallery space would have to be defined in new terms; it would need to be based more on reaching new audiences than on pleasing old patrons and on starting conversations rather than on finishing polished products.

Dialogue as Capacity Building for Social Change

When the Gallery of Conscience team settled on immigration as the topic for its second prototyped exhibition, *dialogue* was both the spark and the fuel that drove the entire process—from concept, to content, to design, to engagement, to action, and back again. Dialogue was not only the primary means through which we invited diverse communities into the museum to engage with each other around relevant issues sparked by the artists' words and works; it was also the primary means through which we engaged community members to collaborate on designing the exhibition experience, selecting the most impactful art, shaping the themes, developing the programs, and organizing for community action.

It all began in the summer of 2013 when we held our first round of dialogues with invited immigrants, refugees, and immigrant descendants from our local communities in New Mexico. Japanese, Nigerian, Tibetan, Mexican, Salvadoran, Korean, Cameroonian, Brazilian, Hispanic, and Indian community members gathered in the gallery, each bringing their own stories, perspectives, and opinions to bear on a wide range of issues surrounding the migrant experience. They discussed everything from racial profiling of newcomers to what it takes to feel welcomed (or unwelcomed) in a new land. The prototyping process we had incubated throughout the previous year assured us that we didn't need fancy bells and whistles to get the conversation started. Indeed, for that first dialogue, we had nothing more than a few color photos of handmade baskets, sculptures, paintings, weavings, culinary dishes, and embroideries made by traditional immigrant artists from throughout the United States. The actual pieces of art wouldn't be installed for months.

The dialogue process itself was one that we had developed through our membership in a special program of the International Coalition of Sites of Conscience, which drew together twenty-seven museums and historic sites from around the country that were focused on immigration issues in their exhibits and programming.[11] We already knew that immigration brings up strong feelings in the public sphere, both personally and politically, and that we had to introduce the topic with sensitivity and care. For example, ask people what they think of when they hear the words "The American Dream" and they can probably tell you personal stories or spout strong opinions, any of which could be slanted positively or negatively. This holds true whether they immigrated themselves, their families immigrated generations earlier, or they were already here when newcomers arrived. In order to create a safe space to allow for these potentially charged conversations, we knew that we needed to start slow, build trust, share commonalities, and graciously explore our differences. Creating a kind of "arc" of experience, the dialogue process was designed to draw participants in as strangers and move us, a few hours later, to understand ourselves as "neighbors." The process opened with introductions and icebreakers, moved to personal stories, escalated to issue-driven discussions, and wound down to sharing lessons learned and calls for action. It is this kind of experience that we hoped, over time, could build capacity within our community for increased understanding, tolerance, and equity. In an article on the power of folk arts to catalyze social change, folklorist Betsy Peterson stressed the importance of dialogue for this kind of social equity work in a civic democracy. She said:

> We may not normally consider dialogue and conversation as capacity building, but they are essential building blocks for cultural capacity building, the kind that builds a sense of confidence, the kind that enables the individual to recognize him- or herself in the collective struggles of others, the kind that can ground true social change.[12]

After an initial icebreaker designed for participants to get to know one another around the universal concept of "home," we dug more deeply into the charged nature of home within the context of immigration through an examination of the artworks themselves. With the photos of artworks spread out on a table in front of them, participants were asked to select a piece that represented "home" to them; then they were asked to work in pairs to share their impressions and reflect on the many ways in which the idea (or reality) of home can be nurtured, challenged, or threatened when we move away or when others move in. Some participants, especially newcomers of color, were moved by the artwork to share stories of being treated with fear or suspicion upon their arrival in the United States, others reflected on a neighbor's gift of kindness or other ways in which they had been welcomed upon their arrival, and all newcomers shared nostalgic memories of home evoked by the images of traditional foods or artifacts from their native lands.

In focusing on two or three of the more "political" artworks offering visual or verbal commentaries on the immigrant experience, we next guided participants to contemplate how people's conceptions of home might be different if they had been forced to leave in a hurry—perhaps under threat of death or persecution, forced to vacate their ancestral lands to accommodate more "powerful" newcomers, or forced into detention centers, jails, or hostile settings as a result of the migration process. "From this kaleidoscope of perspectives," noted our community engagement coordinator and dialogue facilitator Laura Marcus Green, "emerged two core themes, helping us to narrow our exhibit focus on the enormous and complicated topic of immigration: the struggle to belong in a place where you may or may not feel welcome, and the experience of living between two or more cultures." While the artworks sparked the initial feelings and memories, there was nothing particularly unique about them in and of themselves. Rather, what was emphasized in these sessions was the role of the museum as a place where cultural hierarchies could be "revisioned" and where counter-narratives to hate and intolerance could be offered.[13]

Based on these early dialogues, the Gallery of Conscience team crafted an initial iteration of the new exhibition with a title reflecting the unfinished nature of the process and the invitation for audience responses: *Works in Progress: Folk Artists Reflect on the Immigrant Experience*. As with the HIV/AIDS prototype, we opened with a limited number of artworks (sometimes in the form of enlarged photos) displayed on the walls and in makeshift cases, computer-printed label texts and community quotes, two or three mockups of participatory exercises, and an invitation for visitors to explore, participate, comment, reflect, and contribute their thoughts, stories, and voices. Artworks included such pieces as a refugee's embroidered story cloth illustrating the Hmong people's forced exodus from Laos at the end of the Vietnam War, an ex-voto painted as a thank you to Santo Niño de Atocha for the miracle of a mother and her baby surviving sunstroke while crossing the US-Mexico border, a Lakota Sioux beaded cradle created to convey a contemporary social statement about immigration with the words "The Border Crossed Us" beaded across the cradle's top, and an embroidered scene depicting a young Holocaust survivor's first view of the Statue of Liberty from the ship that carried her family to freedom in the United States.

Within the first month of the exhibition's soft opening, we held another set of dialogues in the Gallery of Conscience. This time, we had the benefit of an actual physical exhibition as the catalyst for the conversation. We invited refugee and immigrant community members as well as artists, advocates, activists, and social service providers from within a one-hundred-mile radius. In addition to the immediate impact on the participants themselves and the concrete input we received from them about exhibition design and content, something extraordinary began to happen as relationships were formed, ideas were exchanged, and creative energies were ignited.

Again, the trick was to be nimble enough to recognize what was happening and respond "on a dime."

Our community engagement coordinator Laura Marcus Green was that first responder, drawing on her exquisite skills as an ethnographer and interviewer to follow those creative threads back into the communities and see what treasures emerged. Peterson has described this kind of fieldwork as an "engaged awareness," a practice of careful listening and observation through which the multiple "narratives embedded in daily life" can offer up insights, experiences, and artworks often hidden to the more public eye.[14]

One of those threads ultimately led to a series of new art pieces for the exhibition that had either been created, donated, or recommended by participants in one of our dialogue programs. These artworks included a weaving and a youth-generated film from the Ramah Navajo Weavers Association in western New Mexico, highlighting the displacement of this community by European colonists; a *papel picado* (paper cutting) piece of Our Lady of Guadalupe, in tribute to Mexican workers who perished during the 9/11 attacks and went unrecognized due to their undocumented immigration status; a poem by a sixteen-year-old Mexican American high school student, who reflects on the trauma and struggles of her parents' immigration journey and the discrimination they faced in a new home; a Nigerian Yoruba indigo *adire* (cassava-resist dye technique) cloth whose symbols connect its maker to his home country; and a secular Tibetan *Thangka* painting, depicting a Tibetan man deciding whether to stay in his homeland or flee for safety. This last piece was created in direct response to the artist's participation in the dialogue, where he felt the impact of "political" art pieces for the first time. Although the participant/artist had never before expressed his feelings about the Tibetan exodus through his art, he resolved to create a new piece for the exhibition that reflected the political situation in his homeland and his own feelings as someone caught between two worlds.

The second thread Marcus Green followed led out into the community, where she connected to the exciting work of a number of relevant arts and service organizations and began to explore with them ways in which we might collaborate on programs, projects, performances, and events both within and outside the gallery walls. Navigating these burgeoning relationships required its own kind of nimbleness and its own layer of commitment to the social justice foundation of our incubated Gallery of Conscience experience. Fortunately for us, this was a commitment that was both understood and generously supported by state and government arts and humanities organizations including New Mexico Arts, New Mexico Humanities Council, and the National Endowment for the Arts, which all funded different aspects of these civic engagement endeavors.

The Moral Imperative of the Inclusive Museum

As many cultural critics have noted, the demographic shifts in major cosmopolitan cities caused by widespread migration to the United States have put museums at a new crossroads.[15] While our institutions may not have been historically set up to respond quickly or nimbly to the changing needs of these new communities, some would argue that we have nothing less than a moral imperative to do just that. Reflecting on Gretchen Jennings's question with which I began this article, "What role, if any, should museums play in this national immigration crisis?" I find myself drawn to those colleagues who point out that museums—because they are seemingly *removed* from the manifest political centers of conflict and contestation—are in fact supremely positioned to respond to the increasing nativist reactions against immigrants in our public sphere and have a responsibility to do so. As folklorist and immigrant rights activist William Westerman has written, "Museums have a leading role to play in becoming cultural centers where multiple narratives can be told, where people can find safe spaces for cultures to mix, and where xenophobia can be overcome."[16] The challenge, he continues, "is how to become inclusive and relevant to the framework of civic democracy at a time when larger societies are grappling with strong exclusionist tendencies and fear."[17] He has gone on to suggest four distinct yet interrelated ways in which museums might offer inclusivity as its own kind of capacity building and assistance:

> It can refer to programmatic decisions that integrate community input into the museum's planning. . . . The museum can include a diverse range of people among the desired audience; the staff can be diverse and include people from varied backgrounds, origins, perspectives and approaches; and the museum can reflect a society that is itself inclusive of everyone.[18]

This range of "inclusions" is exactly what was being incubated in MOIFA's Gallery of Conscience throughout our *Between Two Worlds* lab; it was a range that moved beyond the "visitor as consumer" model and toward a model that encompassed the full potential of community-based knowledge production, collaboration, and communication. In other words, the nimbleness toward which we were working was not motivated by a desire to increase the visitor experience alone; we were also, and even more importantly, striving to affect a deeper kind of inclusion of the visitor—and the community member—as a participant in shaping that experience and its intellectual, aesthetic, and emotional content.

The first and in some ways most formal way in which we strove to accomplish this goal was to create a Community Advisory Committee drawn from the dialogue participants we had hosted throughout the previous year. The committee, which consisted of eight to ten members, included immigrant and refugee artists, activists, service providers, and organizational leaders who worked closely with the Gallery of Conscience team throughout the *Between Two Worlds* project to hone its conceptual focus, evaluate potential artworks and participatory exercises, and act as ambassadors in their communities to elicit stories, materials, and contacts. Their voices were literally displayed on the gallery walls, reflected in exhibition design and artifact changes, and featured in community showcases and ongoing community projects.

The second way in which we strove for inclusion beyond the gallery walls was to collaborate with our community partners on the development of strong educational programs, projects, and performances that took advantage of our physical gallery space and resources while also being rooted in community people, places, spaces, and agencies. In every case, our goal was to create a program or project that, from a social change perspective, drew immigrants, refugees, and other underserved community members meaningfully into the museum experience (often for the first time) while simultaneously building communicative competence and capacity within their own communities. None of these projects were one-time "museum outreach" affairs; in every case, the collaborations spanned weeks, months, or years and involved sustained, cumulative work. The projects strove to embody the kind of cultural engagement and participation that Peterson describes as place-based advocacy, "an act of naming, resistance, and critical affirmation for communities whose cultural values, languages, and art forms find little support or recognition from mainstream systems."[19] A sampling of these community projects includes:

- *A multiyear collaboration with Creativity for Peace, a Santa Fe–based nonprofit that holds a three-week summer peace camp and year-round leadership program for Palestinian, Jewish Israeli, and local New Mexican young women*—During the summer of 2014, the GoC and Creativity for Peace collaborated in offering the girls an indigo-batik workshop. This workshop was led by Yoruba immigrant and master *Between Two Worlds* artist Gasali Adeyemo; it resulted in a series of quilt blocks depicting their individual artistic responses to the themes of home, belonging, and living between two worlds (photo 4.4). One quilt block depicted Shabbat candles; another depicted a girl's memory of the olive tree from her grandmother's home with whom she no longer lived. The next summer, 2015, a new group of girls came together with *Between Two Worlds* immigrant artist Catalina Delgado Trunk to learn the Mexican tradition of *papel picado* (cut paper). Using this tradition, the girls depicted symbols of home, peace, and reconciliation.

- *ESL program partnerships engaged immigrant students around the four exhibition themes*—Two local ESL (English as a Second Language) programs (Literacy Volunteers of Santa Fe and Santa Fe Community College) drew on the *Between Two Worlds* exhibition as the catalyst for conversation, vocabulary building, and cultural resource sharing. Classes brought their immigrant students to the museum (many for the first time) and then led dialogues in the gallery. Afterward, the leaders continued these experiences within their classrooms with a number of hands-on activities related to the four exhibition themes.

- *A collaboration with a number of local arts, immigrant, and refugee service centers throughout New Mexico*—This collaboration resulted in organized activities

Photo 4.4. Three-way community collaboration between Gallery of Conscience, Creativity for Peace, and immigrant artist Gasali Adeyemo, in conjunction with the *Between Two Worlds* exhibition project. Young New Mexican woman hangs her indigo-dyed quilt square depicting her symbol of "home" to dry at the end of a workshop led by Nigerian Yoruba adire cloth maker Gasali Adeyemo. Participants included young women from Palestine, Israel, and New Mexico.

and programming around the *Between Two Worlds* themes both in their centers and at the museum. After the first year of museum-based activities, the GoC team created a "folk arts and activity guide" for the agencies to use with their clients throughout the year. As one agency director noted, "This visit to the museum and the *Between Two Worlds* exhibition was the highlight of the entire year for my clients who felt so moved and honored to see their own situations—and their own stories—taken so seriously and meaningfully in such a major museum."

- *A series of radio segments featuring the voices of exhibit artists and area youth around issues of home and belonging*—These interviews were conducted and produced by local area youth and interwoven with their own personal reflections of the exhibition themes (photo 4.5). The audio segments were the result of a several-month collaboration between the Gallery of Conscience and two local arts and service organizations for area youth: Youth Media Project, a Santa Fe–based organization teaching the craft of digital storytelling and the art of listening for a socially responsible world; and ¡YouthWorks!, an organization that creates opportunities for disconnected youth and families in northern New Mexico in order to increase feelings of engagement and value as members of their communities.

- *A spoken word poetry residency*—This residency was led by Albuquerque poet laureate Hakim Bellamy and held in collaboration with the same ¡Youth-Works! participants and Youth Media Project staff members from the previously mentioned project.

The ever-changing Gallery of Conscience exhibition served as both seed and soil for these endeavors, prompting dialogue, engagement, and action on the front end and nurturing the growth, maturation, and flowering of exquisite finished community arts pieces throughout the lab period. In the spring of 2015, the Gallery of Conscience featured five of these projects in a special community arts showcase that included live performances of poetry readings, multimedia art pieces, slide presentations of class projects, discussions around the Creativity for Peace quilt project, sample delicacies from immigrant chefs, and a bead-making workshop that was developed by a local artist in response to the recent detention of asylum-seeking women and children in nearby Artesia, New Mexico. Local arts and service organizations with whom we had partnered also promoted their own organizations at information booths during the event.

In July 2015, when the *Between Two Worlds* exhibition had its second major reopening, the fruits of these projects—poetry books, youth-produced radio segments, the Creativity for Peace quilt, artist statements, and artist conversation pieces—were prominently displayed on the gallery walls, at listening stations, and at dialogue tables throughout the exhibition space. And a dozen participating artists and immigrant chefs were on hand to share their stories and reflect on their journeys. These pieces were not auxiliary outputs of the main exhibition; they *were* the main exhibition. Peterson recognizes the power of folk arts to catalyze such engagements as those noted earlier:

> Folk and traditional arts can also create space for dialogue that enables full and authentic engagement with others. Examples highlight how folk arts organizations and their programs, through dialogue, foster intergenerational connection and understanding; broker conversation, opportunity, and access to resources; and link history to contemporary issues toward deeper understanding.[20]

Immigration Conversations

I would like to conclude with a final look at one of the "inclusive" projects we initiated through the *Between Two Worlds* exhibition. Called the Artist Conversation Project, it seemed to encapsulate both the exhilarations and exasperations of responding nimbly yet meaningfully to contemporary immigrant issues within a museum setting. In the summer of 2014, we held a private workshop for eight participating artists on the day after the first *Between Two Worlds* official opening. Because several of these artists were coming from halfway around the world, we were all meeting together for the first time. Of these eight, two were master-level folk artists whose pieces we had purchased at the International Folk Art Market/Santa Fe the year before; four were artists whose works came into the gallery as a result of their associations with one of our dialogue programs; and two were master-level artists whose topically related work had either recently come to our attention or into our museum collection. The eight artists embodied in their life stories and in their works a range of personal and political points on the immigration spectrum. This spectrum ranged from those who had migrated themselves (either by choice or by force), those who remained behind, and those whose lands and culture were disrupted when Europeans first migrated to this continent centuries earlier. There were six male and two female artists. They included artists from Mozambique and Cuba, immigrants from Mexico and Nigeria, a refugee from Tibet, an eleventh-generation Hispanic artist from New Mexico, and two Native Americans (from the Navajo and Lakota tribes). Discussions ranged from the very personal to the political and covered such topics as the racial profiling of newly arriving Latinos to the United States and newly arriving Mozambicans in South Africa, redefining identity in the face of migrations, living between two worlds, and questions of who belongs in a country and who gets to decide who belongs.

Toward the end of our workshop, we invited the eight participants to join together in pairs in order to continue their conversations with each other through letters or journals, via Skype calls, or by art exchanges throughout the year. The idea was that these conversations would continue in the spirit of ongoing dialogue and exchange that we were hoping to foster through this project. The fruits of their exchanges, like all of the projects we had initiated throughout this period, would make their ways into the new iteration of the *Between Two Worlds* exhibition. The artists would be invited back at the time of the second iteration's opening, after this year of collaboration. Sculptors were paired with sculptors, painters were paired with painters, and fiber artists were paired with fiber artists. Upon leaving the workshop, the Gallery of Conscience team was excited to have planted this seed for our ongoing incubation period.

Six months later, we discovered that not one of the artists had taken even an initial step toward contacting his or her partner artist. Language, time, and distance were mentioned as obvious barriers. However, the barrier that most surprised us resulted from our decision to pair the artists together in what they ultimately considered a forced or false display of curatorial control. Here are some of their responses:

- "I am still stuck in my own thoughts about these issues and not clear how to talk about them with a partner or share them."

- "I can't figure out how to reconcile working on one collaborative piece with a partner when we have such different experiences, styles, and approaches."

- "It's hard to think about translating my thoughts into another person's medium or be in tune with another artist to create a single piece together."

Their responses indicated their frustrations with a project idea that felt both creatively restrictive and unnecessarily controlled by the GoC's "curatorial" team. This is an example of one of the pitfalls of experimental projects that McLean refers to as "a prototype killer." She has written that "it's difficult, if not impossible, to do authentic prototyping if those in charge want to limit the ideas or control the outcomes."[21] Yet the beauty of the prototyping experience, she goes on to remind us, is that "failure" does not have to be the end of an inquiry. In many cases, "failure" is the generative beginning of something brand new and even more meaningful. It is one's openness to discovery that is essential "and the flexibility to be able to follow strange paths that might open up along the way."[22] The key, she wisely intones, is to keep talking. To McLean, "Conversation is the most essential of human interactions. It nourishes the exchange of ideas and, with reciprocity and mutual respect, creates new knowledge and insights. And conversation, I submit, is arguably the most powerful form of participation in which a museum can engage."[23]

With this now in mind, we brought the team of artists back together (or at least those within a one-hundred-mile radius) to share a meal and to talk, listen, and learn more about what they had each been thinking since we had last met together six months earlier. What we discovered was that, while the artists had not physically been in contact each other, they were very much engaged with each other's stories, with the project, with their own exploration of the exhibition's themes and with what one of the artists noted as "the power of folk art as a medium of expression about important social issues." Here are a few of the reflections we heard from the artists:

- "I've been thinking about who I was, why I'm here and my sense of identity."

- "I was prompted by the exhibit and the conversations to write an artist's statement for myself—something I have not been able to do in over 50 years of working as an artist."

- "I've been trying to figure out my own identity and my own story as a Native/ Navajo living between two worlds here in New Mexico."

- "We've all been thinking about our sense of identity/sense of self. This has also prompted thoughts about the ways in which stereotypes about our culture are placed on us by others. I've been thinking a lot about where I belong in the midst of these stereotypes."

As one of the artists astutely summed up, "Maybe the collaboration is happening already in the ways that our conversation and our interaction with each other last July has stimulated our thoughts. Maybe what has happened is not in terms of a joint piece but in terms of the ways our thoughts have been stimulated." So we picked ourselves up, dusted off our "wounded" curatorial egos, and made our way in a new direction, with the artists themselves as our guides. Within the space of an hour, they hit upon a new course of action that felt right and true for all involved. The artists would each create a new artwork for the gallery based on our ongoing conversations, and they would each include a short statement about the ways in which these conversations, and the exhibition itself, had influenced or affected their processes and their pieces. The artworks would be on loan to the museum from the individual artists for the duration of the exhibition and they would be free to sell the pieces to interested buyers upon its close. We arranged a date, several months from that point, when the GoC would host the artists again to "unveil" their pieces to each other, allowing them to share their stories of how the works came to be and what surprised them and each other about the final results. The artists literally left the dinner arm in arm, chatting excitedly about their nascent ideas for their pieces.

When the eight new works were finally unveiled and installed for the second official opening of the *Between Two Worlds* exhibitions, two of the pieces specifically addressed the dangers and the heartbreak of those who attempt to cross "illegally" into a neighboring country in search of a better life. One of the artists, Luis Tapia, was particularly influenced by the national headlines of undocumented women and children from the previous summer and the impact that our ongoing conversations about this issue had had on his artwork. He said:

> I have been thinking a lot about the issue of unaccompanied children coming up from South and Central America, which was so much in the news when we met last July and over the last few months. This piece is part of that conversation about what's happening to people in South America who are coming here in search of a better life.

The piece is a painted wood sculpture depicting a thousand-spined desert cactus laden with some of the most intimate personal items discarded by the women, men, and children who have attempted to cross into this country on foot: a baby bottle, a bra and panties (representing all of the women who have been raped and killed on their journeys), a backpack, and a comb (photo 4.6). Next to the cactus is a partially unrolled

Photo 4.5. !YouthWorks! Student Dacien Villa, left, interviews Tibetan Thangka painter, Lama Gyurme.
Courtesy of Museum of International Folk Art Archives [Exhibitions Collection, Between Two Worlds Series AR.00004.259] and Youth Media Project/Littleglobe. Photo by Laura Marcus Green, 2015.

scroll with the names of men, women, and children who have "disappeared" along the way, never to be seen again; it is a seemingly endless list of thousands and thousands of names. The piece is called *Camino de Sueños/Road of Dreams*. The artist explained the significance of the title:

> The road of dreams stands for all of the thousands of men, women and children who are dying on their road to their dreams. Like the rest of us, they are looking for happiness and a better life. The cactus has collected their dreams and is the place where their dreams ended.

For Luis, the point of his art is not to suggest answers to our most pressing humanitarian crises but rather to start a conversation:

> I present issues to people. I don't have the answers but I do have the questions. I present to the public in hopes that they will open their minds to these issues. The government does not seem to be listening. So we have to go person to person to get the message out. And the way I do that is through my artwork. I don't have the answers; but I think my work is a way to start the conversation.

Photo 4.6. *Camino de Suenos/Road of Dreams*, **2016. By Luis Tapia, Santa Fe, New Mexico.**
Image courtesy of the artist. Photo by Blair Clark.

Indeed, it seems to me that this is the answer to Gretchen Jennings's question, "What role can museums play in this issue?" Museums can be the place to start the conversation, to name the experiences, to remember the disappeared, to affirm our shared humanity, and to give a call for action.

Notes

1. Suzanne Seriff was the first guest curator and later founding director of the Gallery of Conscience at the Museum of International Folk Art in Santa Fe from its inception in 2010 through July 2017.

2. Jennings, Gretchen, "Unaccompanied Children at our Borders: Can Museums Help?" Center for the Future of Museums, July 22, 2014, http://futureofmuseums.blogspot.com/2014/07/unaccompanied-children-at-our-borders.html.

3. Gurian, Elaine Heumann, *Civilizing the Museum: The Collected Writings of Elaine Heumann Gurian* (New York: Routledge, 2006); McLean, Kathleen, "Learning to be Nimble: Museum

Incubators for Exhibition Practice," *Exhibitionist* (Spring 2015): 8–13; Simon, Nina, *The Participatory Museum: A Book by Nina Simon*, 2010, http://www.participatorymuseum.org; Adair, Bill, Benjamin Filene, and Laura Koloski, eds., *Letting Go? Sharing Historical Authority in a User-Generated World* (New York: Routledge, 2011).

4. Katie Zezima and Ed O'Keefe, "Obama Calls Wave of Children across U.S.-Mexican Border 'Urgent Humanitarian Situation,'" *Washington Post*, June 2, 2014.

5. Kathleen McLean, "Learning to be Nimble: Museum Incubators for Exhibition Practice," *Exhibitionist* (Spring 2015): 8.

6. Some parts of this chapter are excerpted from Seriff and Bol's 2017 article "Folk Art and Social Change: The Case of the Gallery of Conscience at the Museum of International Folk Art," in *Folklife and Museums: Selected Readings*, second edition, ed. C. Kurt Dewhurst, Patricia Hall, and Charles H. Seemann, Jr (Lanham, MD: Rowman & Littlefield, 2017).

7. Dr. Marsha C. Bol served as director of MOIFA from 2008 to 2015.

8. This exhibition was guest curated by Suzanne Seriff and featured ten artisan cooperatives from around the world that had won coveted positions in the 2010 International Folk Art Market, Santa Fe.

9. McLean, "Learning to be Nimble," 9.

10. Ibid.

11. For more information on the National Dialogues on Immigration Project of the International Coalition of Sites of Conscience, see http://www.sitesofconscience.org/en/what-we-do/connecting/special-projects/national-dialogues-on-immigration/.

12. Peterson, Betsy, "Folk and Traditional Arts and Social Change." A Working Guide to the Landscape of Arts for Change, Animating Democracy, 2011, http://animatingdemocracy.org/sites/default/files/BPeterson%20Trend%20Paper.pdf.

13. William Westerman, "Museums, Immigrants, and the Inversion of Xenophobia; or, the Inclusive Museum in the Exclusive Society," *International Journal of the Inclusive Museum* 1, no. 4 (2008): 159.

14. Betsy Peterson, "Folk and Traditional Arts and Social Change: A Working Guide to the Landscape of Arts for Change," *Animating Democracy*, 2011, 8, http:// animatingdemocracy.org/sites/default/files/BPeterson%20Trend%20Paper.pdf.

15. Westerman, "Museums, Immigrants, and the Inversion of Xenophobia," 157.

16. Ibid.

17. Ibid., 159.

18. Ibid.

19. Peterson, "Folk and Traditional Arts and Social Change," 5.

20. Ibid.

21. Kathleen McLean, "Museum Exhibit Prototyping as a Method of Community Conversation and Participation," *American Folklore Society*, 2013, http://c.ymcdn.com/sites/www.afsnet.org/resource/resmgr/Best_Practices_Reports/McLean_and_ Seriff_Museum_Exh.pdf.

22. Ibid.

23. Ibid.

DIALOGUE WITH AUDIENCES ABOUT MIGRATION IN THE RED STAR LINE MUSEUM

Bram Beelaert

Introduction

The Red Star Line Museum opened in 2013. It is located in the original emigration station of the Red Star Line shipping company in Antwerp, Belgium. From 1873 to 1934, it shipped approximately two million European immigrants to North America. These immigrants originated from all over Europe and made Antwerp one of the major transit cities for emigrants on their way toward a new life. At the emigrant station, third-class passengers were disinfected and controlled before departure, undergoing procedures that anticipated those at Ellis Island in New York or similar facilities at other American ports of entry. The goal was to avoid deportations upon arrival in America. Shipping companies had to bring their refused passengers back to Europe at their own expense and the authorities in Antwerp wanted to avoid scores of destitute emigrants being stranded in their city.

The Red Star Line Museum tells this story. It is a place of remembrance with a narrative museological approach that focuses on empathy. Here, on the site where history actually happened and through close cooperation with the public, testimonies and life stories are presented in a way that gives meaning to the art, artifacts, and physical collections on display. The museum presents the migration process as a universal quest for happiness to which everyone can relate; it explicitly creates a link between the past and present. With a permanent exhibition that focuses on the immigrant experience (then and now) and with accompanying programs including lectures, debates, days for families, and programs for schools, we encourage a broad and diverse audience to reflect on the meaning of the museum's central story of migration.

In several ways, the museum is calling upon its visitors to share their own migration stories (contemporary) and the stories of their ancestors (historical) with and within the museum. In this way, we are creating a community that feels that it is closely connected to the museum, as well as safeguarding our cultural heritage and emphasizing the importance of how the legacies of our ancestors still affect us today. This has resulted in a unique story that encapsulates the collective memory of a social phenomenon that determined the history of multiple countries tied together by transatlantic migration. More often than not, migrants do not come from the upper classes and do not leave many physical traces behind. Most of those who experienced this migration firsthand have already disappeared, and many of the stories (and knowledge) from these people have also disappeared or are likely to disappear within the subsequent generations. The museum's collection documents the journey, the migration process, and the experience of intercontinental travel between 1840 and 1940. These objects are seen as personal and unique; they are essential to the museum as they complement the stories told about those who traveled from the city of Antwerp.

In striving to tell the stories of these people, our museum understands how critical community participation is to the work that we do. Exhibitions and public programs are consciously developed with the goal of connecting with our visitors through their own experiences or family histories. Gaining information for research and building our museum's collection only happens by building relationships with individuals and communities. The biographical digital databases that have been made available to our visitors at the end of the permanent exhibition feature a way for our visitors to upload and share their own stories. Through this database, they are able to email themselves a link to the app so that they can continue working at home on how they want to share their stories with the public.

This example and other efforts to dialogue with the community are central to the DNA of the Red Star Line Museum both in order to create a strong museum community and to stimulate personal and collective reflections about migration by using everyone's personal or family migration stories as a starting point. The rest of this chapter will describe in detail our policy about interaction and will point out how this affects the cooperation (and amalgamation) of various museum functions. Additionally, this chapter will highlight a few projects in which participation was explicitly used to stimulate public dialogue, indicating some of the challenges we encountered during the process. Finally, this chapter will reflect on some of the possibilities and benefits of international cooperation between migration museums or institutions that focus on migrant stories.

The Goal of Public Participation

Audience participation was important long before the museum was open. In 2007, a committee of international experts defined for the first time a very broad mission statement for the Red Star Line Museum.[1] The particular cases of the Red Star Line shipping company and the emigration history of Antwerp stand for the universal and fundamentally human phenomenon of being on the move. This resulted in a museum concept that centered on the migrant's perspective. At this time, we launched the first public call for testimonies and travel memorabilia from passengers. We were particularly interested in life stories and other biographical heritage information about third-class emigrants; these stories would be used to supplement the predominantly maritime artifacts about the Red Star Line company that were already in the collections of the city of Antwerp. The artifacts that we already had illustrated (for the most part) the luxurious life of passengers with first- and second-class tickets on the Red Star Line ocean liners.

Additionally, from the beginning, we decided that we wanted to put the specific history about the Red Star Line and emigration to the United States in a broader context, and we wanted to incorporate current migration into the exhibition as well. For this, we determined that we also needed to start researching personal stories and testimonies about contemporary migration. As a result, the experiences of third-class passengers in the main exhibition are linked to contemporary testimonies of migrants. Because of all of this, a visit to the Red Star Line Museum entices reflection, calls for recognition, and motivates the visitor to share a personal story. Public participation as described here benefits our museum in various ways: it makes the historical story accessible, it is an instrument for the development of a strong museum community, it is a form of prospecting for research, and ultimately it supports our staff as they continue to build the museum's collection.

This emphasis on personal stories and audience participation highlights the close interconnectedness of different museum functions such as research, collection management, educational affairs, and marketing. As previously mentioned, we are constantly and actively seeking new testimonies, objects, and stories. At the same time that this proactivity increases the participation of visitors in the museum's strategic goals, it also becomes a valuable tool for public relations. Prospecting for unique stories is also naturally an important aspect of our collection-building and research policy. As the visitors' stories provide interesting new testimonies, we have gotten detailed information on migration processes that have not often been found in conventional sources or through previous donations; we save vulnerable but valuable heritage. An additional benefit is that newly acquired stories sometimes become the impetus for temporary exhibitions. For example, from September 2014 to September 2015, we developed a temporary exhibition called *Far from the War? Belgian Immigrants in America during the First World War.* The exhibition was based on five stories of Belgian immigrants in the United States during World War I; three of the five stories had been left in the museum by visitors during its inaugural year.

In order to actively gather stories, we use a mixture of strategies. We often utilize the "Your Story" application, a digital input form with which visitors can upload their migration stories or the story of an ancestor. The resulting PDF can be used for personal or family use after the visit but can also be sent to the museum. This ensures that there is some type of post-visit touchpoint for the visitor and that we are able to potentially prospect for research interests and object collection. If the story is sent to the museum, it is added to our story database, The Warehouse. This database is available for visitor consultation through four terminals at the end of the permanent exhibition; with an emphasis on being user-friendly, The Warehouse serves as a resource center for visitors. People are able to find in-depth information about collections and objects but can also browse through all of the personal stories that have either been recently added or that did not make it into the permanent exhibition labels. And perhaps most importantly, scanning through The Warehouse entices more people to contribute their stories—thus starting the process again.

Just as it is important for visitors to make connections to personal stories in the exhibitions, it is also important for the museum to provide ways to make connections with staff and volunteers during standard visitor experiences. Staff at the ticket office, museum guards, and guides are all committed to creating a visit as pleasant and enjoyable as possible. When someone gets touched by the exhibition and expresses the desire to share a story or make a donation, a museum staff member is expected to make time for that person on the spot. If no one is available, forms are obtainable at the ticket office to leave visitor contact information. As often as possible, we sit together with the visitor and drink coffee in the museum bar while we take note of the story or do the intake paperwork for any objects.

As previously indicated, everything gets registered in The Warehouse, a relational database management system developed by the Red Star Line Museum. Many of the collected objects of emigrants are everyday objects such as a suitcase or a travel ticket. These objects derive a large part of their value from the stories behind them. This is why the Red Star Line Museum developed a specific database management system that could link object descriptions to biographical information and related digital-born documents such as sound files or transcripts of interviews. In addition to utilizing The Warehouse for engagement with our visitors within the museum, it is also used as a management system for the museum staff. For this reason, it was imperative that the database was created according to very stringent scientific and museological standards.

Scientific research of the collection at the Red Star Line Museum is done for better understanding of the Red Star Line company and the museum's collections, to support external communications, and to develop visitor-oriented products such as exhibitions, programs, and guided tours. The academic staff are all very closely involved in visitor-oriented choices and considerations, especially in regard to marketing and educational services. And research is often done in close cooperation with the public. That said, we aim to present all of the objects and stories in the most authentic way possible and in the right scientific context. This means that we look critically at recorded testimonies, especially stories about family traditions or those that are deemed "ego" documents. Our staff needs to be in close contact with all of the involved stakeholders, communicating and justifying the choices we make and providing insights into our various research projects. This is especially crucial when the research yields results that differ from the memory of those directly involved in the project.

Finally, we believe in continuing to focus on the personal dimension of the Red Star Line's history in our marketing because we believe in its universality. We want to appeal to the broadest spectrum of our international audiences while paying special attention to diverse stories in regard to age, social class, family composition, origin, place of residence, and so on. To reach this broad audience, there must be close cooperation among our historians, educational workers, and communications staff. While each person has a unique motivation/approach, they all ensure that the collected life stories are used efficiently and respectfully. This is not merely because of the stories' historical value, but also because of their power to engage people with the museum and its content. Familiarity with the stories and involvement with the community are key to the success of our museum.

Contemporary Migration

While we value the historical stories immensely, the collection of contemporary migration testimonies also holds a very important place in the Red Star Line Museum. This aspect of our collection is essential to giving meaning to the core (historical) story told at our museum; by connecting the past to the present, we provide direct relevance for a contemporary audience that visits the Antwerp museum. With 500,000 residents, Antwerp is a relatively tiny city, certainly in comparison with fully fledged metropolises such as New York City. Yet Antwerp is important because there are some 170 nationalities living together in the city. In aiming to reach such a diverse local audience and because of the importance we attach to individual recognition, it is simply impossible to ignore the fact that many residents of Antwerp have recollections that are comparable experiences to the third-class passengers of the Red Star Line. In the main exhibition, it was important to us to have testimonies of recent immigrants that reflect some of the emotions and experiences of the historical Red Star Line passengers.

A year after the opening of the museum, in 2014, the fiftieth anniversary of immigration agreements between the Belgian, Turkish, and Moroccan governments were remembered. These agreements were the starting point for the biggest migration movement to Belgium following World War II. As part of a nationwide commemoration program, the Red Star Line Museum developed the *Home Sweet Home* exhibition, which was dedicated to exploring the yearly vacation travel of many Turkish and Moroccan immigrants and their children and grandchildren during the summer holidays. Artistic interpretations and observations by photographer Mashid Modjaherin and sculptor Bülent Öztürk were featured alongside testimonies of vacationers and an interactive application that allowed visitors to follow people (via blogs and Instagram) who were on their holiday in real time.

Just as we did with that exhibition, we recognize the importance of working with the public to preserve living memory. We are setting up an oral history project with the aim of collecting testimonies and safeguarding living memory and cultural heritage with regard to immigration to Antwerp after the Second World War. Together with professional partners and nonprofit organizations that are at the center of Antwerp's immigrant communities, we want to find witnesses, interview them, collect relevant documentation about immigration to Antwerp, and add these to The Warehouse.

Working with the public about recent migration is altogether different than the interaction with the descendants of yesteryear's passengers of the Red Star Line. We note that in contrast to the historical stories, people with a recent immigrant past are more reluctant to share their stories. It does not necessarily mean that those visitors don't relate to the historical profiles in the museum. It means that there are more barriers for that specific audience to participate in the workings of our museum, or even museums in general. The Red Line Museum has focused a number of initiatives on recent immigration, highlighting some of the pitfalls and the ways we have dealt with them.

In addition to historical stories, the Red Star Line Museum staff also collected contemporary migration stories from the conceptualization of the Red Star Line Museum.[2]

The aim was to include these contemporary stories in the permanent exhibition in order to complement and give additional meaning to the historical passenger histories. As part of this aim, the Red Star Line Museum converted an old Ford Transit van into a "story bus." Using various interpretive strategies within this story bus, we were fortunate to come into contact with people of diverse origins and ages who had migrated for a variety of reasons. These migrants were able to tell their stories in a conversational atmosphere over a cup of tea and a biscuit. Over four hundred people shared their stories, becoming personally involved in the development of an important aspect of the museum. The bus was decorated in pleasant, warm colors and had retro layout stimulates of the kind that created an intimate atmosphere that was essential to creating a space to make someone comfortable enough to tell our staff the very personal, sometimes happy, sometimes painful stories that are often connected with migration. First, the participants were introduced to the historical Red Star Line story. In this way, the broader context in which their own migration stories would be placed became clearer. This was also an opportunity to forge connections with our future (and hopefully diverse) public. Those who had never heard of the Red Star Line were first shown a short film that illustrated the ways in which Antwerp and its famous shipping company have had a rich history of migration. In this way, the link with the modern migrants' own stories was quickly established.

The first phase of the "story collecting" consisted of an informal interview. Using a list of topics and an identification sheet, we dug deeper into the migration stories of the participants. We looked at potential themes like leaving a home country, taking the journey, the arrival and first impressions, the start of a new life, homesickness, and transformations of identity. This interview was conducted in the language in which the participants were best able to express themselves. After all, it is not easy to express your feelings about a life-changing event like migration in a foreign language! For practical reasons, we decided to limit ourselves to Dutch, French, English, Spanish, Romanian, Arabic, Russian, and Moroccan. These initial interviews were carried out intuitively and were fragmentary in nature. They served primarily as research material to discover which stories and themes often came up in modern migration experiences. And as an added benefit, it allowed us to meet some interesting storytellers. These interviews were not implemented in the traditional manner of a "structured interview." Nevertheless, they still provided us with insights into the themes and inspiration for the potential visual presentation of these stories within the museum's exhibition space.

In a second phase of the interview process, we selected approximately twenty participants for longer interviews. These interviews were recorded in audio, on video, or both. We used a variety of methods to trigger the stories. For example, we have found that photographs are an effective aid in jogging the participant's memory and uncovering details that might otherwise remain hidden. Other elements, such as letters from loved ones and meaningful music, have often had a similar effect.

Eventually, ten stories were recorded professionally for inclusion in the permanent exhibition at the museum. The remaining stories are, of course, accessible via The Warehouse. These recordings have also been transferred to the city archives, partly as a symbolic act that acknowledges that there is a need to consistently (and contemporarily) include the migrant experience in the collective memory of the city of Antwerp.

Fifty Years of Migration

The year 2014 commemorates the fiftieth anniversary of Belgium having signed the 1964 Labour Treaty with Morocco and Turkey. At the beginning of the Golden Sixties, the Belgian economy was booming and was in urgent need of good workers. The 1964 Labour Treaty had an enormous impact on satisfying this need. Countless laborers, and later their families, found new homes in Belgium. To mark the occasion of the anniversary, the cultural sector in Flanders[3] launched the campaign "50 Years of Migration" with an elaborate calendar of events, including theater productions, cooking courses, workshops, and guided walks.

During the summer of 2014, the Red Star Line Museum hosted the temporary exhibition *Home Sweet Home*, devoted to the annual vacations of Moroccan and Turkish citizens in Antwerp to the lands of their families' roots.[4] The focus of the exhibition was on the stories and habits that surround this annual ritual and the significance of the trip for both young people and people of the first generation. We wanted to emphasize the often dual identities and varied sense of belonging that dominates these annual trips. The museum asked the artists Mashid Mohadjerin and Bülent Öztürk to make new works with this theme as inspiration. As mentioned, the aim was to connect their artistic expressions with travel stories and photos on Instagram of Antwerpians who were on holiday at the time of the exhibition.

Photographer Mohadjerin planned to travel along with some families, taking the traditional car route from Antwerp through France, over the Pyrenees and through Spain to Morocco. Soon enough, it proved very difficult (almost impossible) to get people to testify about their annual trips to their lands of origin and to take Mohadjerin along for the drive. Numerous objections and difficulties arose, from very practical reasons like "we go by plane" or "there is not enough space in the car to take an extra person" to more profound and at times distressing objections. Some young people could not believe that there was a genuine interest in their stories of travel, and certainly not from a museum that they did not know or from a society that often denied or disregarded their multiple identities.

Ultimately, Mashid Mohadjerin left for Morocco on her own. With her brother at the wheel, she went on a beautiful general photo shoot that focused on the universality of traveling. Photos from this shoot were then presented in tandem with interviews that had been done with families while they were in Antwerp. All of this was presented in something that resembled an old-fashioned family holiday photo album with old and recent family photos and handwritten accompanying commentary. This gave visitors an insight into the significance of the trips to Morocco and Turkey through the lenses of various generations and from both the individual and family levels.

Because the exhibition was open during the summer of 2014, it coincided with the annual trips of many Antwerpians to Morocco and Turkey. We saw this as a chance for our visitors to experience the travels in real time as well as an opportunity to involve (young) people who would identify with a recent migration experience with our museum. We asked several volunteers to post anecdotes and photos of their summer vacations to their former homelands in real time via Instagram. Collaboration and engagement were crucial for this participatory aspect of the exhibition to be successful; the ultimate success of this interactive initiative was all but certain at the outset. We developed a roadmap to recruit and involve those volunteers from Moroccan and Turkish origin. And we engaged some intermediary figures with authority in the community to post and write about their travels; they served as ambassadors of the project. Then in addition to our volunteers and ambassadors, we made a general call for volunteers in the community. The people who answered the call were offered a photography workshop that immersed them in the world of famous travel photographers and provided them with tips for taking pictures while on their vacations. We partnered with *Al Arte Magazine for Art and Culture from Maghreb to Mashriq and Beyond* for their expertise in social media and the activation of young people for cultural projects. Each volunteer was given a page on the website of *Home Sweet Home* with an announcement of the dates of departure and a link to their personal profiles on Instagram. Finally, the volunteers were given a tour of the Red Star Line Museum and a preview of the *Home Sweet Home* exhibition as inspiration for their future reflections. This experience was instrumental in creating authentic engagement with the museum's community. We succeeded. At the end of the summer, almost 1,500 photos had been posted and eight (both well-known and lesser-known) bloggers had written regularly about their holidays on the website page of *Home Sweet Home*.

Lasting Results

One of the key issues in this intensive process is that, up until then, our efforts regarding contemporary migration had been focused on projects and the development of products—all of this is restricted by limited time constraints. As progress is often slow and tangible results are rarely present from the outset, it is important to continue to cultivate whatever sparks of interest have been generated in order to gain successful lasting outcomes. At this point, the Red Star Line Museum is at the beginning of its focus on a number of long-term initiatives. We are charting recent immigration movements to Antwerp in order to connect the migration, heritage, and artifacts of the Red Star Line with contemporary stories. The ultimate aim is to build a unique collection of testimonies, artifacts, and documentation about the experience of migration of individuals and families through time. Also, we are committed to continuing to engage the public as much as possible in order to engage our community with our museum and to ensure that our museum reflects and shares experiences about migration from as many perspectives as possible.

An early and instrumental partnership during the development of the Red Star Line Museum, and one that we will continue as we engage our community, was the one we have with the Ellis Island Museum. They generously provided us with some eighty transcripts of interviews with immigrants who had departed from Antwerp and had been collected during their oral history project during the 1980s and 1990s. These testimonies were key source material because we were too late to organize large oral history programs ourselves at the time of our conception; the Red Star Line stopped its trips in 1934 and most witnesses have passed away. While we, of course, approached the oral histories critically, we leaned heavily on the wealth of recollections, impressions, experiences, and details about the migration process that were contained in these interviews from the Ellis Island Museum.

In light of how influential these oral histories were to our work, we have felt that contemporary oral histories have been missing for more recent immigration experiences to Antwerp. That is why we are starting an oral history project ourselves, with the aim of capturing the living memory of migration to Antwerp after World War II so that we will have these memories on record for future generations. Specifically, we are focusing on child refugees from World War II onward. At this moment, half of the world's refugees are children, and they are more vulnerable than adults. Apart from the specifics of the period in history they witnessed, themes such as trauma, migration and families, growing up, making choices, and reaching adulthood are both shared and very important to young refugees. There will also be a focus on stories from older people, who reminisce about their youth as a refugee, in order to save the testimonies and memories of these people before they are permanently lost.

It is clear that we want to safeguard an important part of Antwerp's cultural heritage and document an essential aspect of the history of the city of Antwerp. But equally important, we want to make this a participatory initiative, leaning on collaborations with intermediary organizations within Antwerp's immigrant communities to make it truly collaborative. The support of these organizations will also be essential to finding potential interviewees and to smoothly cross some of the barriers that we have previously encountered with the sharing of contemporary migrant stories.

That is why we are currently recruiting what we call "field workers," people from diverse backgrounds, often with a past as refugees who will serve as our researchers and intermediaries with different communities during the project. They will receive a thorough training on oral history, migration history, and museum and heritage practices. They will interview people and archive their testimonies for the museum. They will not be volunteers. To ensure quality and out of recognition for the field workers, they will receive competitive pay for their work. They will also be our first partners with whom we will discuss and begin initiatives and productions based on the collected testimonies. Those initiatives can be within our museum walls or in the city and within communities. We are planning to conclude our project with an exhibition at the museum in 2021, on the seventieth anniversary of the 1951 refugee convention.

A theme like migration, because of its universality, lends itself to international collaboration. In fact, one can wonder if there is any other way to approach migration because a nationalistic approach almost automatically results in a very narrow narrative that is either self-serving to the nation or a tiresome and perhaps dated debate about the benefits or disadvantages of migration.

Migration is inherently linked to the evolution of European societies. Europe's history is one of continuing mobility and the mixing of people across ever-changing boundaries because of migration. That said, the memory of past migrations as a constituent component of European identity has often been ignored or has even been consciously downplayed in order to serve the (erroneous) dominant idea of homogenous nation states throughout Europe. We are glad that there is a growing interest throughout Europe in the conservation, research, and dissemination of the memory of past migrations and the idea interrogating what it means to have a European identity. Half a dozen new migration museums have opened their doors on the European mainland in recent decades. Some of them, mostly located in historic emigration port cities such as Hamburg, Germany; Bremerhaven, Germany; Genoa (Genova), Italy; Cherbourg, France; Antwerp, Belgium; and Gdynia, Poland, focus on the historic emigration of Europeans. Others, like the Musée de l'histoire de l'immigration in Paris, France, DOMID in Cologne, Germany, and Immigrant Museet Indvandringens Kulturhistorie in Farum, Denmark, focus on national immigration phenomena.

Like the Red Star Line Museum, almost all of these institutions collect physical objects, ego-documents, photographs, or digital-born documents (including interviews and scanned files), often tied together by an underlying personal or family migration story. They mostly present these historic collections linked to emigration, immigration, or internal mobility from a local or national point of view. Sometimes these institutions try to link the historical stories and complementary objects to a wider transnational European history of migrations within the continent or between the continent and the rest of the world.

Additionally, in some European countries, national commemoration programs, like the previously mentioned fifty years of Moroccan and Turkish immigration in Belgium and the Netherlands, have stimulated archival and heritage institutions as well as migrant and other civil organizations to collect material and immaterial (mainly biographical) heritage linked to more specific national migration phenomena or the transnational family ties they have created. All of these recent collections have been gathered from different perspectives and with different focuses—sometimes national, sometimes local, sometimes transnational or with a more ethnic orientation. The material outcomes have also been diverse—from entirely new museums with permanent exhibitions to temporary exhibitions, websites, books, and so forth. And the methods that have been developed to collect, preserve, research, and disseminate the "biographical heritage" linked to migration are also widely diverse. As a result, the collections themselves differ considerably—sometimes personal objects linked to the migration experience are systematically collected while other collections consist mainly of archival material or are digital-born, or "immaterial" in nature (for example, audio files of oral history programs).

Of course there are also very interesting similarities in how institutions are collecting. For example, many interactive/participatory methods have been tested to involve European citizens with a migration background in these collection-building efforts. Therefore, we are executing our oral history project with refugees as part of a larger initiative on a European level, involving Amsterdam, the Netherlands; Paris, France; Turin,

Italy; and Westphalia, Germany. Intentions are to build a collection of testimonies, archived by the same quality standards, to explore together the field worker methodology, originally developed in Amsterdam, and to experiment with heritage practices and oral history methodology as a means to stimulate participation of newcomers and refugees in European host societies.

In conclusion, the structure of the European Union makes collaborative efforts between European cultural institutions possible and it should help the institutions to expand their hard work and raise awareness about the issues of migration through a more international lens. Next, one will wonder why we must halt at the borders of the continent. In short, it doesn't have to and isn't halting at the borders of the continent. The partnership between the Red Star Line Museum and Ellis Island Museum culminated in the summer of 2016 when the Ellis Island Museum hosted a temporary exhibition by the Red Star Line Museum; the temporary exhibition will be focused on a shared European and American migration history. After World War II, global migration reached unprecedented heights and will continue to be a major political and societal issue. At the same time, more and more people will be confronted with their own life stories and identities when they leave to pursue lives away from their origin countries, when they see their children off who are going to study in other countries, or when they begin to get to know their new neighbors who speak a different language within the walls of their home. So knowing that migration is a very relevant theme globally, we ask of our fellow cultural institutions around the world—who have you partnered with recently?

Notes

1. Based on the application dossier for obtaining the quality label of the Flemish Government as a cultural heritage organization, as prepared by the Red Star Line Museum team in 2014–2015.

2. Based on Babazia Nadia, "The People behind the Statistics: Modern-Day Migration Stories in the Red Star Line Museum," in *Red Star Line 1873–1934*, edited by Beelaert Bram et al. (Leuven: Davidsfonds, 2013), 115–16.

3. Flanders, where Antwerp lies, is one of the states in federal Belgium. It consist for the most part of the nation's Dutch-speaking territories. In Belgium, culture and education are federalized matters.

4. Based on Babazia Nadia, Beelaert Bram, Devroey Linde, and Lombaerts An, "Levensverhalen en storytelling in het Red Star Line Museum," *Faro tijdschrijft over cultureel erfgoed* 7, no. 4 (2014): 24–31.

WHO IS AN AMERICAN?
Moving Conversations at
Lowell National Historical Park
Emily Levine and Resi Polixa

The chief aim of interpretation is not instruction, but provocation.

—Freeman Tilden, *Interpreting Our Heritage* (1957)

At Lowell National Historical Park, provoking our visitors to connect Lowell's history to their own lives is at the core of our work. We are a unit of the National Park Service, tasked with interpreting the vast history of the country's first major industrial center, now a postindustrial city. Lowell, from the start, has been a city of movers: from the factory women of the 1830s who relocated from the nearby countryside and the Irish immigrants of the 1820s who worked on the city's canals to southern and eastern European immigrants at the turn of the century and modern-day immigrants and refugees from Southeast Asia, Africa, and Latin America.

To further explore the changing nature of life in Lowell, in the summer of 2014, we added a new tour to our regular suite of programs: *Moving Conversations*. This program was a downtown walking tour, focused on the essential question, "Who is an American?" *Moving Conversations* represented both a departure from our traditional interpretive narratives around immigration and from the typical lecture-based tour that we previously provided. *Moving Conversations* was a chance for an alternative space: a program that was intentionally interactive, incorporating multiple points of view and providing space for critical reflection. What follows here is our program model as well as lessons learned from the experience of developing this program.

Laying the Groundwork

Moving Conversations represents a shift in the way Lowell National Historic Park (LNHP) interprets immigration, so developing it required examining our existing interpretive framework and goals. Since its founding in 1978, LNHP has drawn heavily on a "city of immigrants" narrative, primarily interpreted as a majority white, Euro-American collage of cultures that reflects the bulk of Lowell's late nineteenth- to early twentieth-century immigration. The park's 1978 enabling legislation (considered its core interpretive mandate) noted that "the cultural heritage of many of the ethnic groups that immigrated to the United States during the *late nineteenth and early twentieth centuries* [emphasis added] is still preserved in Lowell's neighborhoods."

Following the passage of the Immigration Act of 1965, which dismantled earlier nationality-based quotas, Lowell's immigrant population began rising on a level not seen since the storied early twentieth century. The 1980s saw significant refugee resettlement from Cambodia; today, Lowell's Cambodian American community makes up an estimated 15 percent of the city's population. Latinos represent 17 percent of the population and Lowell remains a major destination for refugee resettlement from Burma, the Democratic Republic of Congo, Iraq, and other nations. In 2010, 22 percent of Lowell's population was born abroad (twice the national average) and only 58 percent identified as non-Hispanic white, compared to 92.5 percent in 1980.[1] Today, Lowell is more a literal "city of immigrants" than it was when the national park was established, but we wondered: Are these newer stories part of LNHP's interpretive mandate? And what does it *mean* to be a "city of immigrants," past and present?

From the chambers of the Lowell City Council[2] to visitors attending park programs, statements around immigration-based demographic change in our city often contain familiar tropes: referencing an idealized immigrant past (a "city of immigrants"), confusion or misconceptions about immigration statuses and policies, connecting local experiences and national politics, citing economic concerns, making demographic assumptions, and discomfort talking about immigration issues in our community. The prevalence of these tropes has made it clear to park staff that exploring recent immigration and modern American identity is critical to our community relevance. Examining continuity and contrast between past and present immigration experiences is essential in interpreting Lowell's transition from an industrial to a postindustrial city—and thus to our interpretive mandate. Visitors and community members frequently invoke Lowell's immigration history in order to comment on its present. We believe that LNHP can be an effective place to work through these conversations, a forum for informing, complicating, and illuminating the past-present link.

Traditionally, much of the park's interpretation of immigration has coalesced around the "city of immigrants" framework, the "bootstrap" narrative of success through hard work, and an ostensibly nonpolitical celebration of diverse ethnic culture—traditional arts festivals and collecting cultural artifacts. At its founding, LNHP rode a larger cultural wave of what historian Matthew Frye Jacobson calls the "ethnic revival" among acculturated, authenticity-seeking white Americans, characterized by an intertwined emphasis on ethnic culture, "bootstrap" mythology, and "state-sponsored heritage." Jacobson highlights an uncritical nationalism in this ethnic revival: the idea that national (and civic) identity is defined and strengthened by its immigrant roots. Yet this framework falls short of engaging with questions of conflict, inequality, and the diverse circumstances of American migration.

Moving Conversations represented a new effort to push back on these simplified—and often exclusionary—narratives. As public historians, we have a responsibility to facilitate encounters with history that integrate the perspectives of visitors from diverse backgrounds. We have a responsibility to do so in a way that values visitors' family histories while questioning assumptions about identity and values that different immigrant groups have brought to this country. With this program, we sought to center the core values of empathy and critical reflection. In its goal to move beyond polarizing or idealized rhetoric toward open-minded, historically based dialogue, this program is not "neutral," as it strives to be a space for diverse points of view.

Getting Comfortable with the Process

For our work group, developing provocative new programming around immigration experiences demanded time and a commitment to *process*—identifying how the process would support our themes and mission, develop the program, and create tools for sharing authority and for self-reflection.

Park interpretive supervisors supported the experimental nature of the process. They supported provocative topics and the dialogue model and assigned six interpreters (the authors included) to a team that would develop and facilitate the program. Members of this group had attended varying amounts of facilitated dialogue training, so comfort with dialogic techniques varied within the team and collaboration was key. We designed *Moving Conversations* as a dialogue integrated into a walking tour; this allowed the staff a basic level of familiarity with the format. Beginning with a basic program outline, the team held weekly meetings to define *Moving Conversations*'s goals, audience, central question, dialogic arc, and tour locations. We spent nine months developing the program for several hours each week, but the lengthy process made it possible to work through our multiple perspectives and collaboratively solve problems.

The first step of the developmental process was to define working goals, which included:

- to expand the conventional narratives around immigration at LNHP and foster visitor connections to Lowell's historic landscape;

- to question the idea of an idealized immigrant past, politicized rhetoric, and intolerance toward contemporary immigrants;

- for visitors to develop a deeper understanding of how ourselves and our communities fit into the landscape of creating American identity; and

- for visitors to practice respectful, dialogic communication on a charged topic.

In reaching for these goals, it was important to management and staff that the "central question" or theme of the program be provocative and hold contemporary relevance. This led us to initially consider questions of immigration *policy*—as we had seen modeled in Ellis Island's programs. Yet we struggled to make this fit Lowell's historical and contemporary identity as a site of settlement, community formation, and cultural transition.

Seeking a central question that would better fit Lowell, we turned to identifying historic resources as "stops" for the walking tour. LNHP's historic properties and exhibits surround Lowell's downtown, and in order to create a strong program, we needed to utilize our surroundings: Lowell's streets, landmarks, buildings, and neighborhoods that reflect the impact of immigration in our city. We initially identified sites in the downtown district where a typical tour would travel. However, just one block west of downtown sits the Acre neighborhood, one of Lowell's largest residential and immigrant-identified neighborhoods—once home to Lowell's nineteenth-century Irish American and other European communities, today the residents of the Acre include many recent immigrant families. A stop in the Acre was important: its small businesses, churches, and historic housing developments are an essential geography of immigrant experiences in Lowell. We began to focus more on the Acre and, in turn, on questions of community identity and experience: *Who is an American?*

In beginning to craft a program around this question, we looked to community sources and collaborators with both academic and experiential knowledge of Lowell's immigration legacy. Staff identified several individuals whose work is aligned with the program's values—supportive of contemporary immigrants to Lowell and connected to the city's immigration history—who could provide critical perspective. We met with staff and clients from a social services agency serving refugees and immigrants to Lowell, who presented on their organization's work and clients' experiences. We invited a local scholar to present a workshop on immigration policy, the politics of American identity, and false disparities between the employment, migration, and language patterns of contemporary immigrant groups and historical ones. Though both presentations were valuable in shaping the content and focus of *Moving Conversations*, future program development will require greater commitment to involving Lowell's recent immigrant community—this will be discussed in greater detail shortly.

Finally, building a capacity for peer feedback was central to our process. For the initial development period, we circulated many iterations of central questions, tour locations, dialogic techniques, and eventually a program outline (via Google Docs and in biweekly meetings) among the interpretive staff, creating a cycle of review, feedback, and change. The interpretive supervisor played an important leadership role in keeping development on schedule and collaborative, focusing our work and making sure each team member was heard. Once we began offering the program to the public, visitor surveys and peer feedback remained a valuable source of knowledge in addressing challenging visitor interactions and developing stronger facilitation skills. And after three months of delivering the program daily, *Moving Conversations* was still evolving, never perfect, and always thought-provoking: "every time I do this program, a visitor points out a way of looking at Lowell that I've never seen before," said one interpreter.

Designing for Self-Directed Learning

Staff intentionally built time into the program plan for visitors to explore and observe. Asking visitors to observe and report back is an effective way to "redefine relevance"—or find personal meaning—in the site. If a visitor has the chance to figure out why a place is personally important (as opposed to the facilitator *telling* them why it is important), that visitor will find a stronger connection to the place and their experiences will be more memorable. Active learning has the potential to create powerful connections that "stick."

Because Lowell's immigration history is so ingrained in the landscape, inviting visitors to be active in their own place-based learning was key to this program. Much of the program (including the stop in the Acre) relies on visitors' observation skills. While we wanted visitors to engage directly with their surroundings, we were concerned about a problematic "gaze" dynamic, in which a ranger in uniform with a group of visitors (possibly visiting from out of town) would be "looking at" the local surroundings and residents' homes. We did not want to foster an "us/them" split atmosphere between out-of-town visitors and local residents and strove to develop questions to focus on personal reflection rather than distanced judgment—particularly as the Acre stop was adjacent to a public housing complex. We asked visitors to remain mindful of the fact that we would essentially be walking through people's homes and to maintain respect of the landscape we would see there.

Defining "group guidelines" to share with visitors at the outset of each program was an important part of the development process and key to setting up the expectation of respect for both the place and for the experiences participants shared during the program. In light of our program goals, we worked to foster a space in which visitors felt safe enough to be able to share their opinions and experiences. A "safe space" is one in which everyone is held accountable to the group in order to build trust and create a learning environment in which no one feels judged, personally attacked, or hurt. A "safe space," however, is not the same as an emotionally "comfortable space": discomfort can be reflected upon, learned from, and interrogated in a respectful environment.

Preparing for Challenging Visitor Interactions

Many of our staff initially found it hard to imagine placing so much control of a tour in the hands of visitors. One particular area of concern with this emotionally and politically charged topic was the potential for combative or "triggering" comments—those that the facilitator or others in the group might find personally hurtful. We found it important to mentally prepare what we might say if a loaded comment hit a trigger—both for ourselves and for other participants. Together, our staff worked through the potential comments that made us nervous to facilitate a program on immigration. What could we say in such instances to keep the space safe? What were measures we could take to preempt such possibilities? We came up with several strategies.

Consider personal triggers and the organization's nonnegotiables and set appropriate guidelines to protect both program participants and the facilitator.

Each of us has our own individual emotions. As public historians and interpreters, we may represent an organization that carries a public stance or an implicit opinion. Trying to work under the pretense of neutrality and objectivity as a facilitator can cause more stress than necessary—it's okay to admit holding opinions on immigration while still striving to create a safe, open space for dialogue. We learned that in a dialogue program, we could protect ourselves preemptively against triggering comments with group guidelines or agreements—provided that they are general enough to work not only for each of us facilitating but for the group as well. That way, if a comment came up that violated the guidelines set at the beginning of the program, the group (not just the facilitator) had a common framework to return to (that is, "I would like to remind everyone of the guidelines we agreed on, in the interest of keeping this a safe space for all of us."). These are some of the guidelines we used regularly:

- "Respect the place": This is a guideline we set at the beginning of programs to guard against value judgments being made about the Acre and its residents.

- "I'd like for this to be a judgment-free zone": We set this as a guideline in order to preempt judgmental comments about participants' personal experiences and perceived backgrounds or about how people identify themselves (that is, "Why can't we just all be 'Americans'? Why do we need labels like 'African American' and 'Asian American'?").

- "Use 'I' statements—speak from personal experience": We set this guideline to prevent against a few different triggers: generalizing about contemporary immigrants, the propagation of stereotypes, or an "us" versus "them" dynamic. Given the juxtaposition of "old" and "new" immigrant communities in the Acre, this guideline is critical in reaching toward the goal of questioning assumptions, idealized histories, and intolerance.

Develop handy go-to responses.

Of course, not everything that could have possibly been said could be anticipated. For those potential moments of surprise or feeling thrown off, we found it useful to come up with go-to responses. We found several of these strategies helpful, depending on the comment and the group dynamic:

- Let the visitor elaborate while you process. (That is, "Would you like to say more about that?" and "Tell me more.")

- Halt the conversation for a few minutes if emotions are high to give yourself and participants a chance to process their thoughts. (That is, "I'm feeling a lot of stress/energy in the group right now. Would anyone like some time to collect their thoughts? Let's take [thirty to sixty seconds] in silence just to take some breaths and process together.") Afterward, ask visitors to each go around and say one word about how they're feeling right now.

- Clarify what they really meant. (That is, "What I heard you say was [summarize]. Is that correct?")

- Defer to the group. (That is, "That's very interesting. Does anyone else share a similar experience or have a different experience?," "Would anyone like to respond?," and "Can anyone imagine a situation where that might not be the case?")

Be okay with inconclusive conclusions.

With this dialogic program, we aimed to ask provocative questions and hoped for visitors to hear, empathize with, and think critically about multiple points of view surrounding American identity, not to make everyone agree. Provocation involves the whole person, intellectually and emotionally, in a place-based program. When a historic place provokes, it becomes immediately and personally relevant—not only in the here and now but also in ongoing visitor reflection after a program ends.

On several occasions, we facilitated *Moving Conversations* and had pointed disagreement within the group. In one instance, a coworker recalls that "the tour-goers held the full spectrum of varying opinions on immigration and they all shared their thoughts throughout the tour. No one person was singled out or attacked, which I had to work very hard to avoid as the facilitator." Another coworker whose participants held opposing views reflected that although "by the end of the program, they still had very different ways of thinking about American identity, they were no longer speaking in combative or binary oppositional terms and had each complicated their own point of view." For us, there was no defined "takeaway" message we wanted visitors to go home with, except for the recognition that there are multiple experiences and truths surrounding immigration and American identity. Under this premise of empathy and critical reflection, ending facilitation at a moment where participants acknowledge differing points of view is okay.

Power Dynamics in Immigration Programs

Moving Conversations has begun to shift how we interpret immigration. Social and political inequality, whether it be economic, racial, or gendered, too often sets up conventional and unfair communication dynamics around immigration, but facilitated dialogue has the potential to resist this. Social inequality has bearing on whose voices are amplified the most in the immigration conversation: some voices are given more legitimacy and credit than others. It also breeds an "us" versus "them" mentality—a dedication to protecting one's own status by excluding or marginalizing those with different experiences. Yet at the same time, the familiar alternative does little to combat this oppression: narratives of celebratory ethnic nationalism contain "an almost absolute erasure of power relations that [make] for a fairly sanitized and happy national narrative: diversity as feast, the nation as smorgasbord."[3]

We realized that the way we speak says a lot about us as individuals and as a society. Creating a program that resists and complicates these narratives means interrupting the authority of dominant voices (often our own, as NPS [National Park Service] interpreters) and boosting marginalized ones. Dialogue lets us practice, imperfectly, liberatory ways of communicating about immigration that move away from lecture or debate and toward equal give and take. *Moving Conversations* aims to boost locations, stories, and visitor voices on immigration not seen or heard on a "traditional" park tour. But how do we work to erode the social inequality that entitles some visitors to feel more comfortable and welcome to speak than others? And how do we counteract the imposing and traditionally authoritative image of our uniforms that can be a barrier to creating a safe space for open dialogue?

Demonstrating a commitment to amplifying others' voices (not only the loudest ones) is one way to start eroding barriers, as is creating multiple ways to enter the dialogue—oral, written, visual, and movement-based. Set and honor group agreements and be forthright: "I have a uniform, but not all the answers. I'll be facilitating your conversation rather than lecturing or seeking right answers." Our process at LNHP has also required staff engagement with examining how our behaviors and beliefs around immigration reflect our personal and organizational privileges; staff development in cultural competency was a start, but the process is very much ongoing. In order to keep building toward a "shared authority" model of anti-oppressive immigration dialogues at LNHP, co-creating and co-facilitating programs with community members must be the next step.

Consider What Is Next

Moving Conversations continues to impact our approach to interpreting immigration and community relationships. By making an interpretive commitment to contemporary immigration experiences, we have opened new opportunities for programming and shifted our audience outreach priorities to engage contemporary immigrant and refugee audiences. This program showed us the urgency of interpreting contemporary immigration and identity with park visitors as well as the necessity of developing future programs in collaboration with recent immigrant constituencies—neighborhood associations, ELL (English Language Learner) programs, and mutual assistance organizations. *Moving Conversations* was an opportunity to begin making connections as a potential collaborator and convener of critical conversations around immigration.

Recently, two organizations have reached out to the park about this programming, in addition to the connections we have initiated. In developing these relationships, working with potential partners to identify mutual goals has been essential. We have common ground with one group in a mutual desire to create a tolerant social climate for new immigrants and refugees in Lowell; with another, we share an interest in storytelling as a tool for empowerment, language learning, and connecting Lowell's past and present. In both cases, park programming can function as a platform for boosting immigrant voices in our community and for putting contemporary voices in conversation with the city's history. The programming emerging from these partnerships has taken the form of pop-up museums, dialogue-based workshops, and a series of live storytelling events.

Community co-creation will be our next step, by partnering with an Acre neighborhood advocacy group to develop and co-facilitate a *Moving Conversation Redux*; for example, we might find more engaging tour locations, facilitate story sharing among neighborhood residents, and direct attention to the Acre's ongoing history in the form of the partner's advocacy work.

The interpretive shifts that began with *Moving Conversations* toward greater representation of recent immigrants and their children, over one-quarter of Lowell's population, involve both core narratives and core audiences. For example, in redesigning our Junior Ranger program in late 2014, we identified using the Junior Ranger activity book as a culturally relevant, ELL-friendly outreach tool with a particular emphasis on connecting new Americans in Lowell with the national park. The foundation of our planning has been to work with community partners who live or work within Lowell's immigrant communities to participate in the development process. Yet making these connections has also meant setting clear expectations and respecting our partner's time and resources; as one community member noted at a meeting, many of the families he works with are in "survival mode."

The experience of *Moving Conversations* challenged LNHP staff to begin to fundamentally shift the way we think about Lowell's immigration legacies, our interpretive methods, and our audiences. It made one thing very clear: Lowell's immigrant families and their complex, evolving stories are central to the interpretive narratives and future stewardship of the national park. This program started that conversation; it is our responsibility to keep it moving forward in collaboration with our community.

Moving Conversations **Condensed Program Model** (one-hour program)
Detailed program model at bit.ly/MovingConversations.

Guiding questions: Who is an "American"? What are the meanings and associations behind this label? Where do our identities and experiences (particularly with communities, neighborhoods, and institutions) fit into this "American" construction, and who has the power to define it?

Introduction (ten minutes)

1. Welcome visitors and introduce self.

2. Introduce program and facilitator's role.

3. Context: *The city of Lowell, like our nation, has been fundamentally shaped by immigration and the experience of negotiating immigrant identities.*

4. Visitors introduce themselves and share what drew them to the program.

5. Ask visitors: **When someone asks you, "Where are you from?" what do you say? When might your answer change?**
   a. Go around or pair up and talk about this with someone else in the group.

6. Come back together, state "ground rules" for conversation (anyone can suggest one):

    a. **Judgment-free space**: We're here to learn from each other, not to pick apart others' identities or experiences.

    b. On this tour we'll be walking through neighborhoods; please be **respectful of residents and of the places** we'll be seeing.

    c. **Speak from your own experience.** Try to use "I" statements.

7. **As we make our way to our next stop, I'll ask you all to think about a question from your** *own* **experience:** *Does where you're from define who you are? How so?*

The Worker Statue (ten to fifteen minutes)

1. **What do you see going on in this piece of public art? What does it signify to you?** (Can use a one-word response technique.)

2. *This statue represents Irish immigrant canal diggers in 1820s Lowell. US-born mill workers lived in company boarding houses concentrated downtown; Irish American canal workers, in contrast, were isolated by mill ownership on the outskirts of downtown.*

3. **Would you say these canal workers were "American"? Why or why not?**

4. **I'd like folks to think back to the question I asked in the Visitor Center: In your own experience, does where you're from define who you are? How?** *Take a couple of minutes to jot down your thoughts on an index card.*

5. Bring the group back together and tape their index cards to the back of a white board.

6. **Thinking about the answers on the index cards here and thinking also about Hugh Cummiskey's experience, what stands out? Would someone share a bit about your response?** *Note: Does anyone define themselves as an "American"?*

7. **Transition:** Because we're exploring questions around immigration and "American" identity today, as we walk to our next stop, **think about the word "American"—is there a particular experience or idea that seems uniquely "American" to you?**

Market and Dummer St. Plaza—the Acre (ten to fifteen minutes)

1. **What stands out on the landscape?** *Visitors often connect to evidence of ethnically diverse businesses and monuments or to earlier history of division between downtown (US-born) and Acre (immigrant-identified) neighborhoods.*

2. *After the Irish, the Acre continued to be a point of arrival for Lowell's many different immigrant communities and for some who continue to arrive to Lowell today from places including Southeast Asia, Central Africa, and the Middle East.*

3. **How is this neighborhood similar to or different from the one you live in?**

4. Before, I asked you to think about the word "American" and whether there is a particular experience or idea that seems uniquely "American" to you. **Think about what might make a *place* or a *neighborhood* "American." Is this an "American" neighborhood? What about your own neighborhood?**

5. **Transition:** Earlier I asked you all to think about how where you are from might define who you are. **Who do you imagine other people think you are? When other people pass you by on the street, do you think those people think *you* are American?**

<u>City Hall Plaza</u> (fifteen minutes)

1. Take just a couple minutes, in silence, to walk around the plaza and observe what you can about this place. Then we'll regroup.

2. After regrouping: **Based on your observations and our discussions today, is this place American? What makes it that way?** (Add to list on whiteboard.)

3. **Looking at our list, does this apply to people? What makes someone "American?"**

4. **Do you think other people perceive you as an American?**

5. **Who gets to decide who's "American" or not? Individuals, government, who?**

6. **Conclusion:** *I'd like to recognize and thank you for diving into tough conversations.*

7. *Optional/additional synthesis or "cool down": I'd like to invite folks to tell us, like we did at the very beginning, where you're from—think about a different way you might answer this the second time around.*

Notes

1. Courtesy of the United States Census. A 2015 search for "Lowell, Massachusetts" at fact-finder.census.gov will yield demographic data from the 2000 and 2010 Census as well as a 2013 American Community Survey.

2. http://www.lowellsun.com/breakingnews/ci_26199087/lowell-city-council-whats-cost-teaching-immigrants

3. Jacobson, Matthew Frye, *Roots Too: White Ethnic Revival in Post-Civil Rights America* (Cambridge, MA: Harvard University Press, 2006), 46.

MUSEO URBANO'S BORDER IMMIGRATION DIALOGUES

Yolanda Chávez Leyva

Beginning in the fall of 2011, Museo Urbano facilitated a series of border immigration dialogues as part of a collaboration with the International Coalition of Sites of Conscience. An award-winning public history project of the Department of History at the University of Texas at El Paso (UTEP), Museo Urbano had its roots in the immigrant neighborhoods of south El Paso, so we were enthusiastic about the new challenge. In El Segundo Barrio, one of the most significant Mexican immigrant neighborhoods in the United States, where Museo Urbano began in a turn of the twentieth-century tenement house, over half of the residents are foreign born.[1] Spanish is heard in public as often as English. Immigration was not an abstract concept to the participants in our dialogues. Many were children or grandchildren of immigrants; some had migrated from Mexico to El Paso directly.

As our mission declares, Museo Urbano "reclaims, researches, preserves, exhibits, and interprets the history of the borderlands, especially El Paso-Ciudad Juárez. In doing so, we foster an understanding of the connections between the local and the global as well as the ties between the past and the present. [Our work] invites visitors to reflect on their own place in history, to think critically about history and to act on that knowledge." Developing immigration dialogues proved to be a challenge that aligned well with our mission.

Piloting the first dialogues on the UTEP campus, we asked instructors in the Department of History to offer their students the opportunity to participate. The day of the first dialogue, one instructor approached me, saying, "One of my students wants to know if the Border Patrol will be attending the immigration dialogue." I reassured the professor that only students would be attending. He informed me that some students were apprehensive because of their own familial and personal stories of crossing the border. Here on *la frontera*, the US-Mexico border, people's relationships with immigration and the Border Patrol are complicated. For some, working for the Border Patrol has long been considered one of the "good jobs" available in El Paso and other Southwestern cities; it comes with good pay and benefits. For others, however, the Border Patrol represents something more worrisome, even intimidating. Over the years, one Mexican American colleague was stopped by Border Patrol officers numerous times walking to campus and asked to provide documentation of his status. I have also been stopped numerous times. I understood the student's apprehension. Even before the first dialogue took place, we learned our first lesson. The emotional safety of our participants was critical.

As we continued facilitating dialogues for the next four years, some on campus and others in the community with our partner La Mujer Obrera (The Woman Worker), we continued to learn about working with an issue that has often polarized our nation and that is controversial in our city and state as well. While the lessons are rooted in our location on the US-Mexico border and in our work with our particular demographic, a city that is 81 percent Latino (a third of whom are foreign born), we believe that the lessons are widely applicable. We share some of these lessons here.

Facilitating immigration dialogues in one of the most significant cities related to Mexican immigration has been intriguing and challenging. Through much of the twentieth century, El Paso served as the most significant port of entry for Mexican immigrants into the United States. As early as the 1880s, local newspapers complained about Mexicans crossing the border. During the Mexican Revolution of 1910, thousands of Mexicans crossed the border into El Paso, fleeing violence or seeking employment and staying permanently or (in many cases) temporarily. Immigration shaped the city economically, culturally, and politically. Its earliest neighborhoods, Chihuahuita and El Segundo Barrio, developed in the 1880s as immigrant neighborhoods. The Cristero War of the 1920s brought thousands more as religious unrest continued following the end of the Mexican Revolution. During the 1930s, widespread fear of Mexican immigrants unsettled the city's immigrant neighborhoods. Southside tenements and businesses were demolished or closed as thousands of Mexicans and their US-born children were deported or repatriated during the Great Depression.

As the United States entered World War II, the outmigration of Mexicans reversed as agricultural employers sought Mexican labor once again. Thousands of temporary workers came through El Paso during the Bracero Program of 1942–1964, a binational agreement between the two countries, which resulted in millions of border crossings by Mexicans contracted to temporarily work in the United States in the agriculture and industry sectors. In fact, the first Braceros entered the United States at the El Paso port of entry in 1942, although the Mexican government did not allow Braceros to work in Texas. The state's history of discrimination and segregation of Mexican Americans worried the Mexican government. This convoluted history of immigration and reverse migration, of welcoming Mexican immigrants and then attacking them, is an essential part of El Paso's history. It is also a fundamental part of the American story.

The southern border is a place of creativity and innovation as well as conflict and controversy. Border crossing and border security have acted as lightning rods, locally and nationally, for decades. In 1992, students, teachers, and staff at Bowie High School brought a class action law suit against the Border Patrol in *Murillo v. Musegades*. Bowie High School was founded in 1927 as the first high school for Mexican American students in the city and is located within sight of the international dividing line. In the early 1990s, the Border Patrol had an increasingly visible presence on the high school campus and its surroundings, often shaping the day-to-day lives of teachers and students. The lawsuit had its origins in a 1991 incident in which Border Patrol officers stopped Ben Murillo, a coach at Bowie High School, on the suspicion that he was not documented; officers pointed a gun at him during their questioning. Other incidents came to light as a result of the court testimony. For example, in 1989, the Border Patrol stopped Bowie student Pedro Garcia, a legal resident who did not have documents with him. As part of the questioning, they handcuffed him, took him to the international bridge, kicked him, and banged his head against a wall. The lawsuit alleged that such incidents were not isolated. As a result of the lawsuit, a court injunction ordered the Border Patrol "to use more than race to stop, question or detain people at or near the school campus."[2] The lead counsel in the lawsuit, the late Albert Armendariz Jr., later said, "You can't just stop anyone because they look like a Mexican."[3]

In 1993, just two years after the initiation of the Bowie High School class action lawsuit, the head of the El Paso sector of the Border Patrol, Silvestre Reyes, implemented Operation Blockade (later Operation Hold the Line) that has reshaped Border Patrol policy along the entire two-thousand-mile border to this day.[4] The morning the operation began, Border Patrol officers were met with people throwing rocks and bottles at them.[5] The operation placed Border Patrol officers within sight of each other along a twenty-mile stretch, closing off many of the crossing areas that had been used for decades. Operation Blockade eventually led to increasing migrant deaths as people tried to cross the border in more remote desert areas such as coming through Arizona. It inspired similar "operations" in California and Arizona. This was the difficult and contested environment in which Museo Urbano developed our immigration dialogues.

As part of the Department of History, we began our dialogues by recruiting college students taking history courses at UTEP. Our students reflected the city's population in many ways. Over 79 percent of UTEP students are Latino and we have the highest percentage of Mexican nationals, more than any other university in the United States. In the city, 81 percent of residents are Latino. Thirty percent of our students report a family median income of $20,000 or less.[6] And in our city, 19 percent of our families live below the poverty line.[7] One can stand on the UTEP campus and look across the border at the hilly crowded Mexican colonias filled with cinderblock houses that are painted white with the occasional pops of bright colors of green, yellow, and blue homes. UTEP is so close to the US-Mexican border that in 2010 a bullet shot in Juárez shattered a glass door at UTEP. El Paso and Ciudad Juárez are divided only by the Rio Grande/Rio Bravo (which is often nothing more than a dry riverbed) and, for a twenty-mile stretch, by a tall border fence.

Facilitating dialogue was new to us in 2011, but we quickly saw its value. Within a couple of years, we understood more deeply that dialogue has the capacity to help us to know ourselves better. It has the ability to create a feeling of belonging. And in times of polarization and anti-Mexican immigrant rhetoric, it has the ability to create a middle ground by planting the seeds of respect and understanding.[8] We began each dialogue by introducing the concept of dialogue as a way for individuals to share opinions, experiences, and even solutions based on their own experiences and what they learned from each other. We presented a set of guidelines that called for respect, confidentiality, and nonjudgmental listening, emphasizing that everyone has the right to be heard. Dialogues based on heated issues such as immigration require that the facilitators create a safe structure within which to hold people's stories, opinions, and emotions. Throughout our years of dialogues, history graduate students have been trained as facilitators, providing important skills to carry over to their work outside of the dialogues.

Our earliest immigration dialogues began with a series of photographs of recognizable local scenes such as Scenic Drive, a winding road across the mountains that divides the city where you can see El Paso, Ciudad Juárez, and southern New Mexico; a photograph of a Border Patrol officer apprehending a man; a scene depicting the drive across the international bridge with the American flag fluttering in the breeze; and a sign announcing in English and Spanish, "Welcome to the United States/Bienvenidos a los Estados Unidos." We asked participants to choose one image from the twenty we laid out and to tell us a little about why they chose it. We knew that, by beginning with localized images it would ground the dialogues in the specific place where participants lived. By allowing individuals to recognize familiar places, it helped relax them and encouraged them

Photo 7.1. Immigration Dialogue at La Mujer Obrera.
Courtesy of Cynthia T. Renteria.

to participate in the dialogue. Living on the border, one quickly learns that local history is at the center of everything, yet there is no such thing as "only" local history. The local is directly intertwined with the national, the binational, and the transnational. This is a lesson that we believe applies to everywhere.

Despite some initial hesitancy, participants quickly shared the stories that the photographs personally evoked. When describing why he chose the image of a Border Patrol officer apprehending a man, one student said, "My mother was here without papers. Now she is a resident but not a citizen. They treat us like criminals. My mother is not a criminal." Another student held the image of the welcome sign at the port of entry, saying, "I don't understand why this is in Spanish. This is the United States." Pointing to the same image, another student stated, "When I see this it is like a contradiction. I don't feel welcomed here. I was born in Spain and when I went to Mexico, I felt welcomed. I didn't feel it when I came to the United States." One student chose the photograph taken from the mountain road looking down at El Paso and Ciudad Juárez. "When you are looking down from Scenic Drive, you can see it's all one community and it's connected. But, when you are down there on the ground you see the differences." It was a poignant metaphor for our dialogues. The individual experiences and stories highlighted the differences among the participants. Woven together, however, their stories created a more inclusive understanding of how complex the issue of immigration truly is. Listening to every other participant in the room allowed each individual to have a mountain top view of immigration.

By 2013, Museo Urbano was ready to take our immigration dialogues off campus and into the community. We partnered with La Mujer Obrera (LMO) to facilitate immigration dialogues in the south El Paso community that was once the garment district of the city.[9] A fundamental question for us as we took the dialogue into the community was about what value the dialogue would have for the community participants. We knew from our previous work in the southside neighborhoods of the city that asking people to participate in a dialogue after an often long and exhausting work day and when they had family obligations was difficult. Lorena Andrade, the director of LMO, asked her staff to attend the dialogues as part of their professional development. Founded with the goals of employment, education, health, housing, nourishment, peace, and political liberty, LMO stressed empowering women by encouraging critical thinking, relying on themselves for solutions, and providing leadership training. As we planned the dialogues, we considered how our dialogue program could reinforce these goals.

Over the course of 2013 and 2014, we held a series of dialogues at LMO, which drew from the surrounding neighborhood and the staff of the organization (photo 7.1). Some dialogues left us motivated to continue our work; others faltered. Our attempt to develop programming based on food as a tool of empowerment for the immigrant community was too long. People's attention was lost, particularly because many had come straight from work. The food we provided was delicious yet took attention away from the dialogue. Our next design for dialogue, rooted in history, ended up being exhilarating.

Working with Lorena Andrade, community organizer Alma Maquitico, doctoral student Cynthia Renteria, and undergraduate intern Cathy Santiago, we developed a program that would create opportunities for participants to reflect on their own stories of immigration while placing them in a national and international context. Because Museo Urbano operates on a shoestring budget, we developed a temporary exhibit by stringing a clothesline between two pillars in our meeting area and pinning laminated photographs of significant moments in the history of Mexican immigration to the clothesline: a map of the area taken by the United States after the US-Mexico War of 1846, a nineteenth-century photograph of a train with Mexican women and men standing alongside it, an image of armed men cooking on a small fire during the Mexican Revolution, and a striking image of a 1930s billboard proclaiming "Mexicans Keep Going. We Can Take Care of Our Own. Chamber of Commerce." We chose images that would portray immigration history throughout the twentieth and into the twenty-first century. The photos were local, national, and binational.

We asked participants to walk up to the clothesline and look at the images, return to their tables, and write about their families' connection to any of these historic moments. As we observed, we were ecstatic about what we saw. Many of the participants came to the dialogue program as part of multigenerational families. We saw grandmothers animatedly talking to their granddaughters, mothers and fathers to their children, and all of them writing down their stories. At the end of this exercise, we asked everyone to take their individual stories and tape them to the photographs that connected most closely. To see the images and the papers with handwritten memories on them was both emotional and gratifying. As the participants discussed their experiences, we could see that the icebreaker had connected family members to each other and family stories to larger histories.

Our final dialogue of 2014 returned to the UTEP campus. That fall day, as a small group of students met to dialogue about immigration, there was some nervousness in the room. Although some students attended classes together, they didn't know each other and they were not familiar with the concept of dialogue. We found over the years that the idea of dialogue was new to most people. Participants, both on campus and in the community, wanted to know what would be produced from the dialogue. Would we record them? Would we videotape the discussion? Reassuring the students that the outcome was as simple (and complex) as sharing their opinions and listening to those of others reminded us that structure and clarity are the basis for safety. Essential to any dialogue, we knew safety that day would be particularly important because we based that day's dialogue on a controversial announcement by President Obama.

Days before the dialogue, on November 20, President Barack Obama's message that he would take action to confront what he characterized as a "broken immigration system" and "to deal responsibly with the millions of undocumented immigrants" had stirred national debate. It represented the perfect focus for a Museo Urbano border immigration dialogue. We began with a reflection question: "Do you think people see you as an American?" It is a question I often ask in my classes, one that sometimes shocks students. There are unspoken incidents that we each experience around issues of belonging and American-ness. Who is and who is not an "American" is a central question of US history. Despite the legal definition of citizenship based on the Fourteenth Amendment, the social construction of "American" has shaped the lives of generations of Mexican Americans. During the repatriations and deportations of the 1930s, as today, US-born children experience displacement when their parents are expelled from the country. The answer to the question is not always obvious. Microaggressions, those small, often unintended demeaning messages that people of color experience, reveal the reality that often Mexican Americans are not seen as truly "American." As students confronted this opening question, their immediate reactions were, "Of course, people see me as American." As the discussion proceeded, however, the complexity of their answers materialized. Some admitted that they felt they were not treated equally as Americans despite their birth in this country.

Following the icebreaker discussion, we viewed President Obama's speech together and then entered into a dialogue in which participants reflected on what they knew about immigration and what they did not know. The dialogue was complex. One student supported the increasing number of Border Patrol officers on the border during President Obama's administration, saying that several generations of his family worked for the Border Patrol. Another student hesitantly talked about her mixed feelings toward immigration policy; her family was composed of both legal residents and unauthorized migrants. Some students crossed the border every day to come to school. Others had lived in the United States for several generations and rarely crossed the border to go to Juárez. I left the dialogue impressed with their willingness to share potentially risky information about their families as well as listening to opposing opinions on immigration.

Museo Urbano's border immigration dialogues taught us a great deal about how to engage both students and other community members with controversial and often very personal issues. Despite El Paso's long role as a port of entry and our large immigrant population, the divisions remain present. High school teachers tell stories of conflict between Mexican Americans and immigrants. Letters to the editor published in our local newspaper, the *El Paso Times*, reflect the opposing views present in the Mexican American community. For example, on May 31, 2010, Lorenzo Arriaga wrote, "I know firsthand that immigrants are hard-working people who love their children and want to provide for their families, just like everyone else. . . . There is too much mean-spirited talk about immigrants, as if they are not human beings." The same day, the newspaper published a letter from Ramon Valenzuela, who asked, "What gives illegal immigrants the right to enter our borders without permission and demand the same rights that are reserved for us citizens?"[10] As the Latino population grows nationally, as the "border" moves to the interior of our nation through the movement of migrants to places that have had little to no Latino people historically, the debates over immigration will change. Dialogue has the potential to help us better understand each other.

As a museum without walls, Museo Urbano had the freedom to hold dialogues in different locations that drew different participants. We also had the challenge of creating temporary exhibits to complement the dialogues. Inspired by the work of community museums, or *museos comunitarios*, which emerged in the early 1970s, we looked for ways to develop exhibits and dialogue programming not simply "for" the community but "from" the community. In 1972, UNESCO called for the creation of community museums. In 1982, the organization asserted the right of communities to "build a collective self, [promote] reflection, criticism and creativity" through museums. UNESCO asserted that community museums strengthened memory and fed aspirations for future generations.[11] We believe that our immigration dialogues were a useful and exciting tool toward these ends.

After four years of facilitating immigration dialogues, we are able to share the following lessons. Dialogues can be emotional and even intimidating spaces. Structure is critical to lessening fear and creating safety. As a consequence, a facilitator who can guide participants and actively support and listen to them is essential. As a university-based public history project, we were able to draw on the strengths of graduate students who understood both the history we were working with and the importance of maintaining a safe space. When we went into the community with our dialogue programming, finding a community-based facilitator was critical to our success. In our case, our facilitator not only had to possess good people and facilitation skills, she also had to be bilingual because our community dialogues were held concurrently in both English and Spanish. The skills of the facilitator must meet the needs of the specific set of participants.

We learned that grounding people in the local and the familiar helps to create safety and encourages critical thinking and reflection. Our icebreaker using local images helped encourage participants to share stories and ideas because the images elicited specific memories. When we asked a group, "What is your experience with immigration?" there was little response. When, minutes later, we laid out the images, participants began speaking with each other and with the group, relating stories and memories about their personal experiences with immigration.

We learned that everyone wants to understand his or her place in history. Drawing from my classroom experience with students who often do not think that history has anything to do with them, the Museo Urbano team sought ways to make those connections accessible. In working with a polarizing topic like immigration, it was particularly important to reframe the perspective away from "us and them" to "where do we all fit in this longer history of migration." Icebreakers such as the clothesline exercise were a simple but effective way to connect our individual and familial stories to the larger historical narrative.

A final lesson came from our training as academic historians. The Museo Urbano team has had the advantage of understanding and drawing on local and global histories because of our academic training as historians and working in a department that has a borderland focus. For sites without academic historians on staff, turning to colleagues in history departments as collaborators can enrich the dialogue.

Museo Urbano's immigration dialogues taught us many lessons about the diversity of opinion and experiences among our participants. We learned about the ways in which living on the border makes our lives different and about the ways in which we are part of a larger societal context. Just as importantly, we learned how to confront our own fears of bringing a controversial subject to the community, on or off campus.

Notes

1. "Segundo Barrio Neighborhood in El Paso, Texas (TX), 79901, Detailed Profile," http://www.city-data.com/neighborhood/Segundo-Barrio-El-Paso-TX.html.

2. Susan J. Tweit, *Barren, Wild, and Worthless: Living in the Chihuahuan Desert* (Tucson: University of Arizona Press, 2003), 106; Timothy Dunn, *Blockading the Border and Human Rights: The El Paso Operation that Remade Immigration Enforcement* (Austin: University of Texas Press, 2010), 40–41.

3. Angela Kocherga, "Border Agents Exempt from New Racial Profiling Rules," KVUE ABC News (Austin, Texas), December 8, 2014, accessed April 2, 2015, http://www.kvue.com/story/news/world/2014/12/08/border-agents-exempt-from-new-racial-profiling-rules/20121543/. Ironically, in December 2014, when the Justice Department announced new guidelines to diminish racial profiling, they announced that the guidelines did not apply to Border Patrol agents in the "vicinity of the border." See guidelines at US Department of Justice, "Guidance for Federal Law Enforcement Agencies Regarding the Use of Race, Ethnicity, Gender, National Origin, Religion, Sexual Orientation, or Gender Identity," December 2014, accessed on April 2, 2015, http://www.justice.gov/sites/default/files/ag/pages/attachments/2014/12/08/use-of-race-policy.pdf.

4. Dunn, *Blockading the Border*, 51.

5. "Special Report Part 1: How Operation Hold the Line Changed the Border 20 Years Ago," KVIA ABC News-7 (El Paso, Texas), December 24, 2013, accessed April 1, 2015, http://www.kvia.com/news/special-report-part-1-how-operation-hold-the-line-changed-the-border-20-years-ago/21963050.

6. UTEP Facts Brochure 2014, 2015, accessed on April 1, 2015, http://universitycommunications.utep.edu/facts/index.html.

7. United States Census Bureau, "State and County QuickFacts," for El Paso County, accessed April 11, 2015, http://quickfacts.census.gov/qfd/states/48/48141.html.

8. Museo Urbano is in the process of developing a dialogue format that will combine concepts of medicinal or healing history with dialogue facilitation. Tentatively named "Macehualtlatolli," Nahuatl for "the common people speaking," this process will draw on traditional Mexican healing practices, the cultural process of "pláticas," and contemporary dialogue to inspire self-knowledge and respect for others.

9. La Mujer Obrera was formed in 1981 by former garment workers and community activists who had been displaced from their jobs as factories moved overseas. Many of the women had participated in the historic Farah strike. The organization promoted the goals of employment, education, health, housing, nourishment, peace, and political liberty. LMO stressed empowering women by encouraging critical thinking, relying on themselves for solutions, and providing leadership training. See Joel Zapata, "La Mujer Obrera of El Paso," *Handbook of Texas Online, Texas State Historical Association*, November 22, 2013, accessed March 26, 2015, http://www.tshaonline.org/handbook/online/articles/ocl01.

10. "Letters to the Editor," *El Paso Times*, May 31, 2010, accessed April 11, 2015, http://www.elpasotimes.com/letters/ci_15194896.

11. United National Educational, Scientific, and Cultural Organization, "Community-Based Approach to Museum Development in Asia and the Pacific for Culture and Sustainable Development," http://unesdoc.unesco.org/images/0018/001899/189902e.pdf.

CONCLUSION
Dina A. Bailey

People immigrate for myriad reasons, and yet I believe that at the heart of the immigration journey lies a sense of hope. Perhaps it is as simple (or as complicated) as a hope for something different. Regardless of the reasons for immigration, the decision to immigrate is rarely one that is taken lightly. It is done with intention, commitment, and determination. I know a number of people who have immigrated to the United States and have been welcomed with open arms. This welcome does not mean that those who have immigrated have immediately found a new sense of "home," but it does mean that their paths may have had fewer bumps. I have known others whose hardships have not ended by simply crossing the border. For years and sometimes a lifetime, they felt isolated and homesick and out of step in America. Many of them have yearned for a sense of community. They might ultimately have found this sense of community through where they decided to live, work, eat, or share their faith. They might have come to align themselves with others who shared their values. Or they might have fully embraced whatever they believed it meant to be "American" and integrated according to this belief.

While people have always immigrated to the colonies and then the United States in ebbs and flows, based on personal reasons or influenced by the contexts of their countries, we must also acknowledge those who were born in the United States and who have remained here. Is there an entitlement (however subtle or blatant) that is implied by being born here? Is there something that those of us who were born into citizenship have that those who immigrated here do not? I would dare to say that some Americans believe this to be true—that those who were born here are somehow entitled to something "different" than those who came more recently or more intentionally. To me, that is an unfortunate lens through which to view the world because, for all intents and purposes, the world has "grown" to be a very small place. Borders move, allies and enemies flip at an astounding rate, the power of economics often has as much influence as the power of governmental entities, and the exchanging of cultural experiences happens on a daily basis because of technology, entrepreneurship, and the relative ease of travel. I believe that we are global citizens—for example, as individuals, we are influenced by and influence others based on the stock market, the speeches and decisions of our country's leaders, and the way in which we internalize what we hear from our media outlets.

Today, fear and entitlement often hide behind decisions that are made to create bigger gaps between "us" and "them" rather than using courage and compassion to make those gaps smaller. We think of "difference" as having a negative connotation instead of seeing differences as aspects we should celebrate. However, there is hope. That is what this book exemplifies. In coming together to better understand each other and build authentic community dialogues, the museums spotlighted here have taken steps to be inclusive. Whether they have ultimately succeeded in their *original* intentions, their efforts are to be commended. Their reflections are to be learned from. I have found inspiration in the journey of these museums. Perhaps most importantly, I find happiness in knowing that the journey is not over; we can each make a conscious choice to continue along the path that the courageous individuals reflected here have forged and continue to forge.

In reading this book, you have accepted a call to action. This is your "so what" moment. So what lessons have you learned? So what responsibility do you feel? So what commitments are you willing to make? I could tell you how my thoughts on immigration have evolved through editing these chapters. I could tell you the practical tips that I have gleaned from the experiences of others. I could write for many more pages and many more days about the relevance I find on a daily basis as I make connections between what the contributors have shared in their chapters and what I see walking down the streets of my city, meeting with various cultural organizations in their respective neighborhoods, and watching the trends of the national news. However, I am not going to do any of those things. From here on out, this journey is *yours*.

The museums who were involved in the National Dialogues on Immigration Project and contributed to this book shared a commitment to spread awareness about historical perspectives, encouraged individual and collective learning, and supported communities through opportunities for safe, open dialogues. They had many "so what" moments along the way because of their commitment to the process. They have shared the practical lessons that they have learned, they have evolved in their philosophies about what it means to be collaborative partners, and they have contributed to the inspiration of others.

Take courage from these messages from others. Then *truly* be the change you wish to see in the world. Do not fear being judged for how many steps you take or how much distance you travel. Instead, find inspiration in the fact that you have taken a step in the first place. As you find your way, share your inspiration with others. Encourage people to walk alongside you. See people through a lens of empathy, actively listen and really hear them when they tell their stories, and fully participate in authentic dialogues. This is true for anyone you come across, but especially true within the context of immigration. Whether you are someone who was born in the United States or someone who moved here after your birth, consider what it means to be a good member of your community. In these final moments as you read the last few words of this book, recognize that this is not the conclusion—it is just a new beginning. Every moment is a new beginning to make a choice that is both empathetic and inclusive. Seize your moments!

SELECTED BIBLIOGRAPHY

Bacon, Barbara Schaffer, Cheryl Yuen, and Pam Korza. *Animating Democracy: The Artistic Imagination as a Force in Civic Dialogue: A Report Commissioned by the Ford Foundation*. Washington, DC: Americans for the Arts, 1999.

Bormann, Tammy. "Facilitated Dialogue: Methodology and Applications." Training presented at a meeting of the International Coalition of Sites of Conscience, Sleepy Hollow. New York, August 9, 2008.

Chesser, John. "Charlotte's Rapid Growth Brings Demographic Changes." UNC Charlotte Urban Institute, February 11, 2011. Accessed February 10, 2014. http://ui.uncc.edu/story/charlottes-rapid-growth-brings -demographic-changes.

Edkins, Sarah. "National Dialogues on Immigration 2014." *International Coalition of Sites of Conscience Publicity Brief*, 2013.

Franco, Barbara. "In Urban History Museums and Historical Agencies." In *Public History: Essays from the Field*, edited by James B. Gardner and Peter S. LaPaglia. Malabar, FL: Krueger Publishing Company, 1999.

Gabaccia, Donna, and Vicki Ruiz. *American Dreaming, Global Realities: Rethinking U.S. Immigration History*. Chicago: University of Illinois Press, 2006.

Garcia, Erica. "Dialogue Program Model Description, National Hispanic Cultural Center." January 2014.

Goldfield, David. "National Dialogues on Immigration Project." Support letter accompanying application to the National Endowment for the Humanities, August 2012.

Graft, Conny. "2013 Evaluation Report for the International Coalition of Sites of Conscience National Dialogues on Immigration Project." December 2013.

Hayward, Jeff. "Connecting a Museum with Its Community." *Curator Journal* 52 (2010).

International Coalition of Sites of Conscience. "Civil Rights Sites of Conscience Workshop Report." July 2009.

International Coalition of Sites of Conscience. "Formative Evaluation Survey on Contemporary Immigration." February 2011.

International Coalition of Sites of Conscience. "Immigration Sites of Conscience Needs Assessment." May 2008.

International Coalition of Sites of Conscience. "Immigration Sites of Conscience Network Seminar Report." August 2008.

International Coalition of Sites of Conscience. "Immigration Sites of Conscience Regional Training Project." Application to the Institute of Museum and Library Services, August 2010.

International Coalition of Sites of Conscience. "Minutes of the Civil Rights Sites of Conscience Workshop." June 25–28, 2009.

International Coalition of Sites of Conscience. "Minutes of the Immigration Sites of Conscience Network Meeting." August 8–13, 2008.

International Coalition of Sites of Conscience. "National Dialogues on Immigration Project." Application to the National Endowment for the Humanities, August 2012.

International Coalition of Sites of Conscience. "NEH Planning Team Meeting Agenda." February 2011.

International Coalition of Sites of Conscience. "NEH Planning Team Meeting Minutes." February 2011.

International Coalition of Sites of Conscience. "Network Descriptions." Accessed December 18, 2014. http://www.sitesofconscience.org/networks/asia/.

Jackson, Maria-Rosario. "Coming to the Center of Community Life." *Mastering Civic Engagement: A Challenge to Museums*. Washington, DC: American Association of Museums, 2002.

Jacobson, Matthew Frye. *Roots Too: White Ethnic Revival in Post–Civil Rights America*. Cambridge, MA: Harvard University Press, 2006.

Leyva, Yolanda. "Dialogue Program Model Description, Museo Urbano." January 2014.

Lowell National Historic Park Staff, "Moving Conversations Program Model Draft, Lowell National Historic Park." January 2014.

Mock, Brentin. "Hate Crimes against Latinos Rising Nationwide." *Southern Poverty Law Center Intelligence Report* 128 (Winter 2007).

Moran, Lyle. "Lowell City Council: What's Cost of Teaching Immigrants?" *Lowell Sun*, July 22, 2014. Accessed March 14, 2015. http://www.lowellsun.com/breakingnews/ci_26199087/lowell-city-council -whats-cost-teaching-immigrants.

Nicholson, Freda, and W. Richard West. "Forward." In *Mastering Civic Engagement: A Challenge to Museums*. Washington, DC: American Association of Museums, 2002.

Parmar, Priya, and Shirley Steinberg. "Locating Yourself for Your Students." In *Everyday Antiracism: Getting Real about Race in School*, edited by Mica Pollock. New York: The New Press, 2008.

Passel, Jeffrey S., and D'Vera Cohn. "Unauthorized Immigrants: 11.1 Million in 2001." *Pew Hispanic Center*, December 6, 2012. Accessed February 10, 2014. http://www.pewhispanic.org/2012/12/06/unauthorized -immigrants-11-1-million-in-2011/.

Pettigrew, T. F., and L. R. Tropp. "A Meta-Analytic Test of Intergroup Contact Theory." *Journal of Personality and Social Psychology* 90 (2006): 751–83.

Richardson, Deborah. "Dialogue Program Model Description, National Center for Civil and Human Rights." January 2014.

Rosenzweig, Roy, and David Thelen. *The Presence of the Past*. New York: Columbia University Press, 1998.

Suro, Roberto, and Audrey Singer. "Changing Patterns of Latino Growth in Metropolitan America." In *Redefining Urban and Suburban America: Evidence from Census 2000*, edited by Bruce Katz and Robert Lang. Washington, DC: Brookings Institution Press, 2004.

Tilden, Freeman. *Interpreting Our Heritage*. Chapel Hill: University of North Carolina Press, 2007.

United States Census Bureau. "2000 Census." Accessed February 9, 2014. http://www.census.gov/2000census/ data/.

GLOSSARY

Accessibility: is about giving equitable access to everyone, along the continuum of human difference, ability, and experience. (American Alliance of Museums DEAI Task Force)

Coalition: a collection of different people or groups working toward a common goal.

Colorblind Racism: is the belief that—despite overwhelming evidence to the contrary—race is not a significant factor in determining how opportunities, benefits, and burdens are distributed across the country's population; that all Americans have an equal opportunity to achieve the "American Dream." (www.KirwanInstitute.org)

Dialogue: a focused and intentional conversation, a space of civility and equality in which those who differ may listen and speak together. (www2. clarku.edu/difficultdialogues/learn/index.cfm)

Diversity: is all the ways that people are different and the same at the individual and group level. (American Alliance of Museums DEAI Task Force)

Equity: refers to the fair and just treatment of all members of a community and requires an intentional commitment to strategic priorities, resources, respect and civility, and ongoing action and assessment of progress toward achieving specified goals. (American Alliance of Museums DEAI Task Force)

Inclusion: refers to the intentional ongoing effort to ensure that diverse individuals fully participate in all aspects of the work of an organization, including decision-making. (American Alliance of Museums DEAI Task Force)

Implicit Bias: refers to thoughts and feelings that we are unaware of or mistake about their nature. We have a bias when, rather than being neutral, we have a preference for (or aversion to) a person or group of people. (www.perception.org)

Racial Anxiety: refers to the heightened levels of stress and emotion that we confront when interacting with people of other races. People of color experience concern that they will be the subject of discrimination and hostility. White people, meanwhile, worry that they will be assumed to be racist. (www.perception.org)

Racial Literacy: refers to noticing and lessening the racial fears and the stressful reactions that teachers, parents, and students experience when they face racial conflicts.

Racial Microaggressions: the brief and commonplace daily verbal, behavioral, or environmental indignities, whether intentional or unintentional, that communicate hostile, derogatory, or negative racial slights and insults.

White Privilege: the concrete benefits of access to resources and social rewards and the power to shape the norms and values of society that whites receive, unconsciously or consciously, by virtue of their skin color. (www.world-trust.org)

INDEX

AANM. *See* Arab American National
 Museum
ACCESS, 37n1
active civic engagement: facilitated dialogue
 for, 5; museums and timeline for
 responsive, 65, 70
activity journals, 62
admittance policy, immigration, 16–17
advocacy voices, 4; artist and youth need for, 81;
 dialogues for, 108; language barriers and, *50*
African Americans, 20; America immigrant
 nation excluding, 15; Immigration Sites of
 Conscience Network with sites on, 7–8
African Regional Network, 2
America as nation of immigrants, 16–18;
 African Americans and Native Americans
 excluded from, 15; equal access implied by,
 14
American citizens: global citizen compared
 with, 17; US history central question as,
 118–19; "Who is American" and, 101;
 "Who is Texan?" in, 19
American identity, 15–16
Americans for the Arts, 6
American Southeast and Southwest, 12
Angel Island Immigration Station, 14, 16–17
Animating Democracy Initiative, 6
Antwerp, 99n2; Ellis Island Museum and, 96–
 97; migrant destination as, 89, 93, 95–96

Arab American National Museum (AANM),
 17, 37n3; for all immigration studies, 36;
 Arab Americans as history stewards for,
 29–30; *Connecting Communities* from,
 27, 31; cultural heritage as core value of,
 26; diversity respect of, 26–27; ICSC
 founding member as, 37n10; inauguration
 of, 25–26, *26*; *Little Syria* from, 27, *28*;
 Patriots and Peace Makers from, 27; *What
 we Carried* from, 27; *Women in Time of
 War* from, 27
Arab Americans, 37n1; AANM history
 stewards as, 29–30; Arab American
 National Museum on citizens as, 17;
 history books excluding, 29; as Muslim,
 25–26; stereotyping since 9/11, 25, 29; in
 US as of 1528, 25, 29, 35
Arizona State Museum, 19
Artist Conversation Project, 82–86
artists, 87n8; Artist Conversation Project
 for, 82–86; immigrant communities and,
 15; immigration thread and folk art of,
 76, 77; restrictions and control on, 83; on
 unaccompanied children, 84–85, *86*; youth
 voices included by, 81. *See also* Museum of
 International Folk Art (MOIFA)
Artspace, 37n2
Asian Network, 2
Atlanta History Center, 20

ABOUT THE CONTRIBUTORS

Anan Ameri, PhD, is a scholar, author, activist, and community organizer. Since arriving in the United States in 1974, Dr. Ameri has founded two national organizations: the Palestine Aid Society of America, which focuses on empowering women in refugee camps in Lebanon and the Palestinian occupied territories, and the Arab American National Museum, a cultural treasure and a trusted resource about Arab American history, culture, and contributions.

Bram Beelaert, born in 1978, studied history and journalism. He has experience as a researcher, archivist, oral historian, and publicist. He is currently chief curator and head of research at the Red Star Line Museum in Antwerp. Located in the original buildings of the historical Red Star Line shipping company, the museum revives the story of the line and its passengers and contextualizes them in the universal human migration experience.

Linda Blanshay, PhD, is director of program development at the Museum of Tolerance, Los Angeles. She does partnership development, program design, evaluation, and special projects. She is a dialogue facilitator and offers professional development workshops. Prior to this, she taught university courses in the sociology of inequality, social movements, and intersectionality.

Janeen Bryant, founder of the Facilitate Movement, is a community engagement specialist and catalyst for building organizational capacity. Formerly vice president of education at the Levine Museum of the New South, her work focuses on the power of interpersonal communication, the impact of shifting demographics on visitor interactions, and experiential learning activities to make social change history relevant and accessible to any learner.

Emily Levine began her career at Lowell National Historical Park in 2006. She holds a master's degree in museum education from Tufts University and currently works for the National Park Service in San Francisco. Her professional interests include audience-centered interpretation, training interpreters, and interpreting contemporary issues in historical context.

Yolanda Chávez Leyva, PhD, is a public historian whose work focuses on the US-Mexico border. She is the director of the Institute of Oral History and the founding director of the Borderlands Public History Lab at the University of Texas at El Paso. She is cofounder of Museo Urbano, a museum of the streets, and has published on Mexican American and borderlands history.

Sarah Pharaon is the senior director at the International Coalition of Sites of Conscience, where she directs the coalition's work in North America. From 2010 to 2014, she led the National Dialogues on Immigration, which linked sites across the country in hosting dialogues on contemporary immigration issues affecting their communities. Sarah worked as the director of education at the Lower East Side Tenement Museum and was the founding curator of the Arab American National Museum.

Resi Polixa holds a BA in history from Mount Holyoke College and an MA in public humanities from Brown University. Their interests include social history, community collaboration, interpretive media, and coaching and training interpreters in twenty-first-century interpretive pedagogy. They currently work as a park ranger at Lowell National Historical Park.

Suzanne Seriff, PhD, is an anthropologist, museum curator, and public sector folklorist, dividing her time between her home in Austin, Texas, where she holds a position in the Department of Anthropology at the University of Texas at Austin, and nationwide consultation on innovative museum and community engagement projects at the intersection of arts and social justice. From 2010 to 2017 she served as guest curator and founding director of the Gallery of Conscience at the Museum of International Folk Art in Santa Fe, New Mexico.

ABOUT THE EDITOR

Dina A. Bailey is the CEO of Mountain Top Vision, a consulting company that focuses on organizational transformation in nonprofits. She works with organizations to embrace strategic initiatives that lead to more diverse and inclusive communities. The focus of her most recent work has centered on fostering empathy. Dina worked as the director of museum experiences at the National Underground Railroad Freedom Center and was the founding director of educational strategies at the National Center for Civil and Human Rights.